MANAGING
FORENSIC
TOURNAMENTS

PAUL HUNSINGER
Chairman of the Speech Department
University of Denver

DONALD R. TERRY
Director of Forensics
The University of Toledo

ROY V. WOOD
Associate Dean
School of Speech
Northwestern University

NATIONAL TEXTBOOK COMPANY • Skokie, Illinois 60076

Preface

This manual has been prepared to meet the ever increasing demand for more detailed instructions in the direction of the various types of forensic festivals and tournaments. Each year the number and variety of such meets increase. They are prevalent in every part of the nation from late August until June. Forensics is now a year around affair. The active high school or college team often attends thirty or more tournaments in a year. In some areas of the country, schools send large groups of contestants to several tournaments in one two-day period. The "national high school debate circuit" is approaching the college and university in far ranging travel. For instance, the 1969 Glass City Holiday Tournament at the University of Toledo drew eighty teams from Florida to Texas to South Dakota to New York.

As the number of tournaments has grown, the problem of maintaining and standardizing the quality of tournament management also has grown. Through no fault of their own, otherwise highly qualified people have been called upon to direct a forensic tournament without the benefit of previous experience. Often the results have been good, but anxiety and confusion have certainly taken their toll among new debate coaches.

In addition, the experienced tournament manager has often found himself cut off from communication with his colleagues over ways for improving his tournament. Too busy to worry about new techniques before the tournament—and too tired to care afterward—many tournament directors merely follow the same old procedure. The "old hand" runs his tournament well, but perhaps not as efficiently and painlessly as he might.

In most fields, new and old hands alike can turn to "the literature" to find helpful procedures and suggestions, but this is not the case with the tournament manager: his area of interest has been largely ignored. Although speech teachers have long been concerned with the theory and the practice of participation in forensic events, no one has taken the time to record their ideas on the management of speech tournaments.

Brief chapters in most of the recently published books on debate discuss the tournament, but often these chapters are meant primarily to guide the coach and the contestants as they participate in the tournament, rather than as an explanation of how the tournament should be planned and managed.

It was with this problem in mind that the authors of this manual undertook the task of setting down their ideas on these matters. Although the best way to become a good tournament director will always be to learn through experience, cumulative experience should be shared with other tournament directors and with those who are just beginning. This book is a compilation of ideas and forms the authors have developed over the years, and is combined with many observations of their colleagues' tournaments.

In addition to presenting the background material necessary for understanding modern tournament structure, this text attempts to detail the tasks that confront the tournament manager. It also suggests ways to fulfill the managerial duties efficiently and successfully. The Appendix, "The Tournament Director's Master Notebook," is the major device for fulfilling the managerial duties. The authors have found that a notebook that contains all of the vital tournament information and materials can be the foundation of a highly successful forensic tournament.

The authors also have found that a successful tournament is a coordinated group effort. The text, therefore, is designed to serve as a textbook for students and as a guide for a cooperative adventure in forensic activities. By including his students in the cooperative adventure, the director maximizes not only his chances for a "perfect" tournament but also the educational value of the tournament. By helping conduct a tournament, the student learns not only the skills of speech-contest management but also learns to handle the problems and tensions that are part of every tournament.

Future forensic directors must come from the current forensic programs, and involving students early contributes greatly to their professional readiness.

In addition to providing much more detail, this revision has expanded the number of examples, illustrations, extemporaneous topics and methods, ballots, discussion agenda and included an extensive set of packaged debate schedules. Also, time schedules for various purposes, new types of tournaments, tie breaking examples in debate, individual events and festivals, as well as means of dealing with the double entry type of scheduling have all been added.

It is our hope that more of our present and future forensic direction courses will include this vital data.

Contents

CHAPTER 1

Types and Goals of Forensic competition

THE FORENSIC FIELD

Tournaments and festivals have long been accepted as important parts of the educational pattern in America. Even in the times immediately after the Civil War, schools met each other for verbal jousts on the forensic field. For many years the early, two-school type of competition was the primary form of interscholastic speech activity, but this pattern has been supplanted in recent years by large tournaments that involve as many as a hundred schools, traveling thousands of miles to vie for top honors.

A typical tournament includes many different types of forensic events, such as debate, oratory, extemporaneous speaking, and oral interpretation; or such events as impromptu speaking, discussion, after-dinner speaking, radio and television speaking, and newscasting. Some tournaments and festivals also include subdivisions of a major event; for example, oral interpretation may be divided into interpretation of prose, interpretation of poetry, or interpretation of drama. Some tournaments emphasize debate while others emphasize individual events. Finally, there are those that attempt to strike a balance.

Most forensic coaches believe that the tournament is the best method for gaining the maximum learning experience from debate and other speech activities. Schools throughout a particular area, or from all over the nation, can join in large tournaments to test the ability and knowledge of their students. Limited only by the talent of individual students, most schools find that forensic tournament competition provides an arena in which students can learn this skill and can compare their progress in learning with students from many other schools. Unlike athletic and band competitions, large numbers of students and great amounts of money are not required to "field a champion."

Many educators also have found that a well-run tournament or festival provides many side advantages and values. Guests learn much more than forensic skills and values and the hosts of the competition gain much more than pride or satisfaction in a well-run tournament. The goals, values, and purposes of forensic tournaments and festivals will be dealt with at the end of this chapter, but first it is necessary to define tournaments and festivals and examine the forms they typically take.

WHAT IS A TOURNAMENT?

Although there is general agreement on the common definition, it is necessary to make the meaning of "tournament" very clear. A tournament is a *competitive event* or *series of events* in which participants are *evaluated* to determine *comparative positions* by *ratings*, and *ranks*. The *goal* of a tournament is the *ranking* of participants in each event, according to which the host will award trophies or certificates for the various places.

The element of competition is often controlled by establishing divisions that are based on qualifications, so that novices need not compete directly—at an unfair disadvantage—with experienced persons. In many meets, the best teams and individuals ultimately compete against each other in elimination rounds leading to a final, championship round.

The evaluation of the participants is made by qualified critic-judges who provide the tournament director with the ballots from which he can determine the final ratings and rankings.

"Comparative rank" is usually used, along with a "rating" system. The rankings are made on a first, second, third, and fourth basis; the ratings are usually superior, excellent, good, fair, and poor. There should be a correlation between the ranks and the ratings, but it is possible to give contestants the same rating, although not the same rank. For instance, if the critic or judge decides that three persons are superior, he can give three superior ratings, but he must rank the contestants first, second, third, etc. Rankings, therefore, are more important than ratings. On the debate ballot, both teams can be given the same rating, but each speaker should be ranked differently—from one to four—the teams should have different point totals.

WHAT IS A FESTIVAL?

In organization and management, the festival is somewhat different from the tournament. A festival is a *competitive event* or *series of events* in which participants are *evaluated* to determine *comparative ratings.* Festivals do not emphasize competition and winning because the participants are not ranked; participants are judged against a qualitative subjective standard to determine whether their performance has been superior, excellent, good, fair, or poor. Certificates usually are awarded to participants who received superior and excellent ratings. When more than one round is involved, the decision is reached by averaging, as in the example below.

Although the major difference between tournaments and festivals is in the nature or basis of the awards process, often there are differences in the elements they emphasize.

FORENSIC FESTIVAL

Contestant Result Sheet

Rating

Contestant	RD. I	RD. II	RD. III	RD. IV	FINAL RATING
A_1	Excellent	Superior	Excellent	Good	Excellent
A_2	Good	Good	Fair	Fair	Good*
B_1	Superior	Superior	Fair	Fair	Good
B_2	Excellent	Excellent	Good	Superior	Excellent
C_1	Fair	Fair	Good	Fair	Fair

* Giving the student the benefit of a balanced 2–2 situation.

If both ratings and numerical points are given on a set standard (such as below), the results may be tabulated in this manner.

FORENSIC FESTIVAL

Contestant Result Sheet

Standards: Superior 26–30, Excellent 20–25, Good 15–19, Fair 10–14, Poor Below 10.

Rating

Contestant	RD. I	RD. II	RD. III	RD. IV	FINAL RATING
A_1	Excellent 22	Superior 26	Excellent 20	Good 15	83 Excellent
A_2	Good 15	Good 17	Fair 11	Fair 11	54 Fair
B_1	Superior 29	Fair 14	Fair 14	Superior 28	85 Excellent
B_2	Excellent 22	Good 19	Excellent 21	Superior 26	87 Excellent
C_1	Fair 14	Fair 14	Good 19	Fair 14	61 Good

The festival stresses training and providing experience, and puts less emphasis on competition; and the manager of a festival often provides a feature that is comparatively unique to his festival. Often there are demonstrations or lectures or discussions about forensics. Festivals also tend to schedule more time for each round, to allow ample time for oral critiques after each participant's performance.

TYPES OF TOURNAMENTS

Tournaments evolve to fit the needs of particular speech forms, geographical regions and the interests of individual coaches and there are perhaps fifty or more variations of the tournament format. This section, however, is concerned only with the five most commonly used kinds of tournaments: (1) the novice tournament, (2) the practice tournament, (3) the best-record tournament, (4) the elimination tournament, and (5) the championship tournament. All five types of tournaments nevertheless have several common elements.

The events that are offered form the first common characteristic among the five types of tournaments. Debate is generally the basic forensic event, and at some meets opportunities are provided for the contestants to enter one or more individual forensic events. By offering competition in oratory, oral interpretation, extemporaneous speaking, and other individual events, the tournament can give the student an opportunity to practice and sharpen his skills in different kinds of activities—in addition to debate.

The second common characteristic is the determination of those who will be allowed to participate—on an "open", qualification or an "invitational" basis. Many tournaments are "open" for participation to anyone who cares to come to the tournament and pay the required fees: the coach who wishes to attend with his team need only write for information to be invited.

The educational value of the tournament can be viewed from two sides. If the host has adequate rooms, divisions can be added providing for pairing of schools on a more equal educational level, i.e. years of experience, success, etc. However, the elitest idea of tournaments should be left to the qualifier. If a director has very limited space, he would be best advised to have an open tournament with a narrowly specified division on an experience basis.

As the number of applicants for tournaments continues to increase, however, and as more directors try to improve the quality of their tournaments, many contests have become truly "invitational." The tournament director, in the latter case, invites only the schools he feels will contribute most to the overall tournament. In order to receive an invitation, applicants typically must ask to be put on the waiting list for future invitations. Tournaments are now developing, such as the Tournament of Champions, to which only those schools or teams qualifying by certain achievements are invited. Even the high school circuit is developing such contests.

A number of "league" tournaments—the fifth common element of the major formats—are held every season. State and national high school honoraries, for example, hold both state and national championships. In addition, several college-level tournaments are held each year, either for league or forensic fraternity members. Admission to a league or fraternity tournament must be preceded by an application for membership, by writing to the appropriate administrative officer, usually the executive-secretary.

Now that the common elements have been discussed, we will turn to the details of the *types* of tournaments. The *novice tournament* is just what the name denotes. Almost every forensics coach has found that one of the most difficult parts of his job is teaching the techniques of forensics to students who are new to the activity, and it is difficult to find "outside" competition for such students. Although they need the challenge of facing students from other schools, they may soon become discouraged if they have to compete against more experienced people. The novice tournament, therefore, is a training program, and the critics or judges usually give the contestants oral comments on their performance after each event.

The novice tournament's emphasis is on methods of improvement rather than on winning. Therefore the tournament manager who offers either a fall novice tournament for those who have just become interested or a spring novice meet for students who developed an interest late in the season will usually find that he has a large number of applicants. An excellent substitute for the strictly novice tournament is a novice division meet, with room for many entries, that is held along with a regular meet. Here again the tournament director must recognize his room limitation problems. If he has space perhaps a novice division could be scheduled with less rounds than a more experienced division. This would allow for less pressure and for more valuable instructional time for judges.

EXPERIENCED—NOVICE SAMPLE SCHEDULE

Experienced Division		*Novice Division*
Round I	9:00 a.m.	9:00 a.m.
Round II	10:30 a.m.	11:00 a.m.
Round III	1:00 p.m.	2:00 p.m.
Round IV	2:30 p.m.	4:00 p.m.
Round V	4:00 p.m.	

This type of schedule will also help to alleviate pressure on luncheon facilities by allowing for a more staggered lunch hour.

The *practice tournament* is usually held in the autumn because even the most competitive coach prefers not to enter his teams in stiff competition early in the season. To prepare his teams for more difficult competition later in the season he needs a tournament that provides a learning atmosphere, where students can try new approaches and cases without fear of losing "The big one." He needs a tournament in which qualified judges have sufficient time to criticize techniques and to discuss the case analyses with the participants. Many schools, therefore, provide one-day practice meets during October weekends, and also may schedule such contests on the "off" weekends during the regular season. Managers who offer practice tournaments throughout the season offer the strong argument that, although competition has many educational values, the competitive process is enhanced by providing practice meets.

The importance of the practice meet should not be overlooked. Often this tournament may be of a local or regional nature and need not be of the high powered trophy, prize winning variety. It has become the practice in some states to award trophies. However, in others, the awards are only the satisfaction of learning about the topic and procedure of debate from other teams and critic judges. This may be one of the ways to help combat the pervasive influence of the "trophy hound."

As participants and coaches begin to feel a need to ascertain the best speakers and schools, they often turn to the *best-record tournament*. Here, the tournament manager typically offers six rounds of debate and three rounds of individual events, on a Friday and Saturday. The tournament winners are determined by comparing the records of the teams and the individuals to find those who won the most debates or received the highest rankings in individual events. Even if he is forced to reduce the number of rounds because only Saturday is available, the tournament host can easily provide a good balance between competition and learning. The skilled participants can go all-out for the awards (and still learn a great deal in their own right), and the less experienced participants can have a number of rounds of tournament competition in which they can gain experience and sharpen their skills.

In the *elimination tournament*, every effort is made to find the top participants in each event, In debate, after all of the teams have participated in five or six rounds, the best teams are selected for final rounds. Usually, the eight most successful teams are chosen for quarter-finals, with the winners moving on to semi-finals and finals. Three or more judges usually are used in each round to assure the best decisions. In individual events, two to six contestants face each other. Obviously, elimination tournaments are best suited for that time in the season when teams and contestants have fully developed their cases and presentations. Novice contestants are entered in elimination tournaments, but it is not wise until late in the season, but a non-elimination novice division may be run concurrently with the elimination events.

Some may argue that the *championship tournament* is merely a "glorified" version of the elimination contest, but the quality and competition of such a tournament often make for a very different kind of experience. The purpose of the championship tournament is to find the most proficient speaker-contestants in a league, a region, or in the nation. The tournament director will offer six to eight preliminary rounds in debate, and often these rounds are judged by more than one critic. The sixteen best teams may then be chosen for the octo-final round. By the time the final round has been decided, one can assume that the champion—or at least the team with the most endurance—has indeed been found. In large, championship, individual events contests, the procedure in some areas is to offer two or three preliminary rounds, after whch only the first-place speakers proceed through the eliminations. Among the other possibilities are: the National Forensic League system where contestants speak until they have two downs; and the five or six preliminary rounds are followed by quarter-finals, semi-finals, and final rounds. (This down means ranked in the lower half of his section.) The eliminations proceed until only 6 or 7 students speak in a final round.

TYPES OF FESTIVALS

Although there are many sound arguments for the educational value of direct, forensic competition, many speech educators also believe that the less-competitive festival situation is worthwhile. If we remember that the primary distinction between the tournament and the festival is that the latter makes no attempt to rank contestants, but only to give awards on the basis of ratings, it is possible to identify three general types of festivals: (1) the forensic festival, (2) the individual events festival, and (3) the discussion festival.

In the *forensic festival* the manager has a great deal of freedom in choosing the events he will offer. He might limit the events to debate, or he might offer several individual events in addition to debate. He can offer four to six rounds of debate, and two or three rounds of individual events, and easily arrive at a determination of the speakers who should be given certificates for excellent and superior performances.

Many festivals are limited to *individual events*. A festival, for example, might restrict itself to interpretive events, and the oral-interpretation festival might offer divisions in drama, poetry, and prose, or it might become even more specialized. Some meetings might be labeled "Shakespeare Festival," "Modern Poetry Festival," "American Literature Festival," and the like. Group interpretive events might be offered in a "Readers' Theatre Festival" or a "Chamber Theatre Festival."

Generally, competitive participation in group discussions has been replaced by *discussion festivals* or contests that give the speech student valuable experience in cooperative inquiry. Group-discussion events are particularly well suited to the festival format because many coaches have found that an attempt to rank discussion contestants often results in a competitive atmosphere that subverts the cooperative atmosphere that is necessary in group inquiry.

The festival may be structured for maximum learning experience by providing for critiqued demonstrations such as illustrated in this example:

PROPOSED FESTIVAL SCHEDULE

Friday November 1

1:00–2:00 p.m.	Registration
2:00–2:30 p.m.	General Meeting
2:30–3:30 p.m.	Interpretation, Oratory, Discussion, Demonstration and Critique
4:00–5:15 p.m.	Round I Interpretation, Discussion and Oratory
5:15–6:15 p.m.	Extemp—Impromptu Demonstration and Critiques
6:30 p.m.	Draw for Extemp and Impromptu
6:40 p.m.	Impromptu Round I Interpretation, Discussion and Oratory Round II
7:15 p.m.	Extemp Round I

Saturday November 2

8:30 a.m.	Debate Demonstration and Critique
10:00 a.m.	Round I Debate Round III Interpretation, Discussion and Oratory
10:00 a.m.	Draw for Extemp and Impromptu
10:10 a.m.	Round II Impromptu
10:45 a.m.	Round II Extemp
11:30 a.m.	Round II Debate Round IV Interpretation, Discussion and Oratory

12:15 p.m.	Draw for Extemp and Impromptu
12:25 p.m.	Impromptu Round III
1:00 p.m.	Debate Round III Extemp Round III
2:00 p.m.	Draw for Extemp and Impromptu
2:10 p.m.	Impromptu Round IV
2:45 p.m.	Debate Round IV Extemp Round IV
4:30 p.m.	Festival Results

Discussion as a festival event should be treated as a form of cooperative learning experience. The format should be clearly spelled out, the students should be placed with entries from other schools, and the entire procedure should look towards problem solving.

Example

ROUND I   What is the problem?
    A. Definitions
    B. History of the problem
    C. Scope of the problem
ROUND II   What are the causes of the problem?
ROUND III   What criteria should be utilized to select a solution?
ROUND IV   What are the possible solutions and how do they measure up to the criteria?
ROUND V   What is the best solution and how should it be implemented?

OTHER TYPES OF FORENSIC EVENTS

Speech education is carried on in most schools through formal classroom work and extracurricular speech activities, and often these can be combined—within the school—so that classroom instruction is supplemented by a kind of speech-tournament experience. For instance, the classroom teacher may decide to hold an *intramural forensic contest* as a means of increasing class motivation and as a technique for getting non-speech students interested in forensic activities. Because an intramural contest can be conducted in the same way as an interscholastic tournament, it is not necessary to elaborate on this type of event. Teachers who offer an intramural program can also offer regular forensic events and can follow many suggestions that are offered in this text as guides for contest management.

The intramural contest can be established in two ways. It may be a single tournament event at a specific time in the school year or it may be a progression of events during the academic year. For maximum educational benefit, the progression of events will allow more students more opportunities to participate more widely and help to sustain interest. The format can be class against class, organizations against organizations, or simply individual participation. However it is arranged, the competition must be fairly and competently directed with a goal in mind.

Another type of forensic event is the *congress* whose general format follows that of the legislative assembly. Students organize political parties and working committees to prepare resolutions and bills, and this is followed by parliamentary debate, as in a general or legislative assembly. Although we will not deal with the management of a parliamentary congress, this type of assembly is highly recommended for a well-rounded and exciting experience in many of the forensic activities. The director of a congress needs ample facilities and a good parliamentarian to be well on the way to operating a successful assembly.

Values of the congress are numerous and many states and leagues are adding separate congress competitions. To host a congress, the following are necessary:

1. Large and comfortable assembly rooms for each house of the congress.

2. A determination of the number of houses and qualifications for each.

3. A means of allocating representation among invited schools.

4. Bills and resolutions for debate chosen in advance and sent to delegates.

5. Stop-clocks—stop cards—pages, ample ditto paper, ditto machines, committee rooms and faculty advisors.

For complete details see the National Forensic League manual on student congress. It is available by writing the national office in Ripon, Wisconsin.

We have shown that the teacher who wishes to host a forensic meeting has a large number of types of contests from which to select. He can choose any one of several types of tournaments or is almost unlimited in the kind of festival he can offer. Most prospective contest hosts carefully examine their reasons for holding a meeting, as well as the wishes of their prospective guests, before they decide upon the form their tournament or festival will take. The remainder of this chapter is devoted to a consideration of the various goals that can be met by the several different types of speech meetings.

THE GOALS OF THE TOURNAMENT OR FESTIVAL

Obviously, there may be as many purposes for tournaments and festivals as there are people who design and attend them. A good contest is one that fulfills the purposes of the group in attendance and the purposes of those in charge of the encounter. Conversely, a poor tournament does not achieve its goals, or seems to have no purpose. The goal of the tournament or festival is the basis for one's operational philosophy and method of organization. Not only should the purpose be clearly stated at the outset, it also should guide the entire operation.

When a formal or informal organization of coaches and educators plans a forensic program for the entire year, the purpose of the tournament or festival is often determined by such a group. Tournaments, however, have a way of becoming traditional, and often the original purpose is forgotten. The tournament director should take the responsibility for checking on the purpose and on the need for the tournament. There will be various purposes, of course, but the tournament director should find the *common* purpose and direct the tournament accordingly.

The common purpose can often be a combination of the ones discussed below and should be clearly spelled out in the initial announcement. Many tournaments are *not* planned by a regional group, but are simply offered at the option of the host institution. Therefore, such goals should be clear to all who choose to attend.

The three general goals that hosts and most contestants aim for in speech competitions are (1) the type of forensic experience to be gained, (2) educational experience and value, and (3) victory. Although every tournament obviously will contain elements of all three goals, different types of tournaments at different times of the year result in greater emphasis on one or another goal.

Early in the season, tournaments often are designed primarily to provide forensic experience, and coaches enter students who need to try their forensic skills in front of impartial judges. Coaches also have orators who are just beginning to formulate their speeches, which later will be polished. And they have new debate team members who—primarily—need tournament experience, and oral interpreters who will make their first presentations. The emphasis in this type of tournament is on providing sufficient rounds for diversified experiences while leaving the schedule open in order to allow ample time for critiques by the best possible judges.

Frequently the focus is on the educational values to be gained from a tournament. Contestants may or may not be experienced but they attend the contest so that—in an atmosphere of learning—they can try their best cases and finest ideas to see how they hold up. If these values are the focus, the forensic festival usually is "the answer." Certificates of quality are awarded, and sometimes trophies. Rounds are scheduled to allow for ample critiques. Discussions between teachers and students provide a classroom atmosphere for a non-competitive but concentrated experience.

The critique period must be viewed by coach, critic, and students as a learning—teaching situation. The critic must take copious notes, be skilled in analysis, and willing to treat every contestant as his student to coach for that hour. The student must approach the critique as a valuable opportunity to gain another qualified coach's view of his case and his technique. The demonstration debate-critique at the outset is most valuable. A schedule such as this example might be most effective.

Sample Schedule

8:00– 8:45 a.m.	Registration
8:45– 9:00 a.m.	General meeting
9:00–10:00 a.m.	Demonstration debate
10:00–11:00 a.m.	Demonstration critique
11:15 a.m.	Round I
1:30 p.m.	Round II
3:30 p.m.	Round III

Eventually the focus will be on competition. As the forensic season progresses, students and coaches alike begin to wonder which schools have the best teams and the best contestants in individual events. Because they want the satisfaction of beating these rival schools, the tournament therefore changes from a casual to a highly competitive experience. Critiques may not be given; schedules are arranged so that weak teams will be eliminated and only strong teams will emerge.

After the tournament manager has determined the primary goals he wants to attain, he is ready to structure a tournament that will promote these goals. The following chapters, therefore, deal with the tasks he must perform and offer suggestions on how they can be done most efficiently.

CHAPTER 2

The Direction of Forensic Competition

THE GENERAL NATURE OF THE MANAGEMENT TASK

The prospect of managing a forensic tournament or festival can be absolutely terrifying. The manager must plan to carry on voluminous correspondence with the prospective participating schools. He must make all advance arrangements for publicity and hospitality. He must know how to set up rounds in several events in such a way that students have a fair balance of competition, and see that students do not meet each other more than once. No critic can be allowed to judge his own students or judge the same students twice. The manager must also secure ballots, maps, trophies, instruction sheets, time cards, and other important materials and have them ready as needed. Arrangements for rooms and meals must be made well in advance of the tournament. All this and more must be done in addition to the tournament director's normal teaching load; usually he must manage his tournament or festival in his "spare time."

Like many other complicated enterprises, however, the multiplicity of details will seem less frightening and complicated if the tournament manager fully understands the nature of his role as host of the contest. If he has scheduled his tournament with a definite purpose in mind, if he understands his position in the organizational hierarchy, and if he knows, in general, what the guests are looking for, the tournament can be turned from a nightmare into a dream.

THE ROLE OF THE TOURNAMENT MANAGER

The tournament or festival manager is the key man in the organizational structure but he should not try to do everything by himself. Many tournaments have been ruined by a director who, because he didn't trust his students or didn't want to share authority, tried to perform every detail of the operation. If a tournament manager tries to schedule judges, timekeepers, rooms, and tabulate all of the results, he'll soon be so busy that he will not be able to work effectively. There are just too many jobs for one man to handle. The director should divide his responsibilities and delegate them. Even after he has done this, he will have four major roles to perform: educator, supervisor, coordinator, and public relations expert. Let's take a look at each of these.

EDUCATOR. The tournament director is a teacher, first and foremost. He conducts an educational program for persons in forensics and educates his students in managing a competitive forensic event.

Because education is in many ways a unique or personal experience, each student will gain something different from the experience. One student may learn about general organizational procedures while another may learn how to handle people in crisis situations. Others may simply develop appreciation for the problems and complexities of the tournament or festival—and later think twice before they complain about a tournament they are attending.

It must also be remembered that the tournament manager is the director of a larger educational experience, that is, the tournament itself. He provides the setting in which students can receive more speaking experience in a single day than they would normally get in a semester-long speech class. He also provides the setting in which the students are not taught by a single teacher but have the benefit of the advice of competent critics from many different schools.

The tournament director, therefore, should take the educator's point of view in all his work. His purpose should be primarily the education of students, which he accomplishes by providing the best possible atmosphere for learning.

SUPERVISOR. Although the director must delegate many duties and responsibilities, he must take final responsibility for everything that is done. It matters not that a room problem was caused by the failure of a janitor to unlock a door or prepare a room; the manager will be the one who is blamed. No matter how his staff performs, it will ultimately be considered a reflection of his abilities. For this reason, and for the obvious reason that he has management and leadership experience, the director should supervise and guide the work of his staff. He should know who can be depended upon and who needs helpful watching. He should personally check the most important details, such as the tabulation of results, but leave the less important details to be handled by others.

COORDINATOR. Because of his vested responsibility and the needs inherent in the situation, the tournament manager should have an overview of the entire tournament. From the first letter to the awarding of the last trophy, he will plan and supervise the tournament's development. He coordinates the work he has delegated. He brings the efforts of his students and helpers together at the proper time and place so that the tournament is a unified and meaningful whole.

The tournament director: educator, supervisor, coordinator, and public relations expert.

The best system or device the authors have found for tournament coordination is the *master notebook*. A tournament director can compile such a notebook, for his personal use, that contains a copy of everything that pertains to the tournament: final schedules, rules and regulations, judging assignments, and all other relevant materials. He can use this notebook to review or help solve the problems that arise, to answer questions, and to plan the steps of the tournament. The master notebook has been found so valuable that the authors have provided a detailed description of it at the end of this chapter and a sample master notebook as the Appendix to this manual.

PUBLIC RELATIONS EXPERT. The tournament director must work with many groups other than just participants and their coaches. He must develop good working relations with the administration and staff of his school. Support for and pride in the tournament or festival from the entire host school can be great assets in presenting a successful contest. The tournament manager also must cultivate good relations with the community and the press. The former is often a source of qualified judges and provides support for a tournament. The latter is an obviously valuable tool for pre-contest publicity and for announcing the results of the competition.

Unless the school has a functioning public relations office that excludes his doing so, the director should *personally* visit each of the news media and persuade them of the news value of the tournament. The public relations functions call for the most tactful, helpful, responsible actions on the part of the director. His greatest asset is his willingness to help, his accuracy and promptness in reporting, and his desire to be a "friend" to the news media representatives; to facilitate their responsibilities; and to relate to others in the community.

These four roles of the tournament or festival manager—educator, supervisor, coordinator, and public relations expert—are vital for meeting and fulfilling the various management tasks. Like the managers of other enterprises, the contest manager is faced with a set of jobs that must be done and is confronted with the task of applying the proper procedures to see that they are completed. Our attention will now be given to a detailed analysis of specific management tasks. Then the master notebook will be discussed to show how it can help coordinate the procedures. The other chapters of the manual will be devoted to the procedures the authors have found most effective in meeting the demands of the various tasks.

SPECIFIC MANAGEMENT TASKS

As has been mentioned, the first task of the manager is to determine the *goals and purposes* of his particular speech contest. At the very outset he must determine the kind of emphasis he wishes to place on the educational and competitive aspects of forensic events. Although these two goals are not mutually exclusive, a tournament can be structured to emphasize one or the other.

After the goals and purposes have been set, the director is in a position to define the *nature of the contest*. He will decide if he will hold a tournament or a festival. He can determine whether he wants his contest to be open to all who wish to enter or if it should be restricted and invitational. He can, finally, select the events he will offer in his competition.

The next task is the preparation of a *tournament announcement* that includes the information essential to those who plan to attend the contest. A *list of events* must be provided, along with a set of the *rules and regulations* that will govern these events throughout the contest. The announcement also must specify the *number of contestants* that may be entered by each school in each event. The *deadline for entry* also must be specified, along with a statement of the penalties that will apply to those who are late in meeting the deadline. The tournament announcement also explains the *fee structure* for the contest, as well as the *judging obligations* of the visiting teachers. An *entry blank* must be included and should be designed so that it contains all of the essential information. Finally, the announcement may contain *visitor information*, such as a list of hotels and motels, a map of the city, a map of the campus, and a brochure of activities of interest in the host city.

EXAMPLE OF TOURNAMENT ANNOUNCEMENT

GENERAL INFORMATION

1. *Events:* The following events will be offered this year: debate, extemporaneous speaking, oratory, and oral interpretation.

2. *Limitations:* Each school may enter two debate teams, three participants in extemporaneous speaking, three participants in

oratory, and three participants in oral interpretation. A contestant may enter debate and only one individual event.

3. *Entry Fees:*

Debate .... $5.00 per team

Individual Events .... $2.50 per entry

4. *Judging:* Each school is asked to provide a qualified judge. If this is impossible, there will be a $25.00 fee, which will be used to hire a substitute.

This is generally modified to one judge per debate team (2 or 4 man) and one additional judge for each 5–7 individual entries.

5. *Awards:* Trophies will be awarded to the first two places in debate and to the first-place winners in each individual event. Certificates will be awarded to all debate semi-finalists and to the top three places in the individual events. A trophy will be given to the sweepstakes winner, selected on the following basis:

Debate:

1st place —7 points

2nd place—5 points

3rd place—3 points

Individual Events:

1st place —3 points

2nd place—2 points

3rd place—1 point

6. *Deadline for entries:* All entry blanks must be postmarked no later than *January 31, 1970.* Due to space limitations, we cannot grant participation to schools submitting late entries. Changes in registration may be made by phone up to noon on February 9.

RULES AND REGULATIONS

Debate

Proposition: The national topic will be used.

Rules: Traditional style: two persons on a team, each speaker presenting an eight-minute constructive and a four-minute rebuttal. Each team will debate both sides of the proposition.

Procedure: Each school may enter two debate teams. There will be one division of debate. The four top teams in the preliminary rounds will be selected to debate in the elimination rounds on the basis of win-loss record and speaker ratings.

Extemporaneous Speaking

Subject area: Topics will be drawn from current affairs since September, 1969.

Rules: Contestants will draw three topics thirty minutes before speaking, selecting one of them for a five-to-seven-minute speech. Notes may be used. All contestants should report to their sections at the start of each round.

Procedure: There will be two preliminary rounds and a final round. Contestants will be selected for the final round on the basis of ratings and rankings.

Oratory

Rules: All orations must be the original work of the contestant and must not have been delivered in competition prior to September. Orations are limited to ten minutes maximum. Delivery may be from memory or manuscript.

Procedure: There will be two preliminary rounds and a final round. Contestants will be selected for the final round on the basis of ratings and rankings.

Oral Interpretation

Topics: Round I   Twentieth-Century American prose

Round II   Twentieth-Century American poetry

Procedure: Selections should be six to eight minutes in length. There will be two preliminary rounds and a final round. Contestants will be selected for the final round on the basis of rankings and ratings. The Round II selection will be used in the final round.

PRELIMINARY SCHEDULE

February 9

6.00 p.m. to 9.00 p.m. . . . . Registration (Business Adm. Bldg.)

February 10

9.00 a.m. to noon . . . . . . Registration (Business Adm. Bldg.)

Noon . . . . Extemp. Draw

12.30 p.m. . . . . Extemp., Interp., and Oratory Round I

1.30 p.m. . . . . Extemp. Draw

2.00 p.m. . . . . Extemp., Interp., and Oratory Round II

3.15 p.m. . . . . Debate Round I

4.30 p.m. . . . . Debate Round II

5.45 p.m. . . . . Debate Round III

February 11

8.30 a.m. . . . . Debate Round IV

9.45 a.m. . . . . Debate Round V

11.00 a.m. . . . . Draw for Extemp. Final

11.30 a.m. . . . . Finals Individual Events

1.00 p.m. . . . . Results and Awards

1.30 p.m. . . . . Semi-final Round

2.45 p.m. . . . . Final Round

ENTRY FORM

Debate: Team 1

1. ....

2. ....

Debate: Team 2

1. ....

2. ....

Extemporaneous Speaking

1. ....

2. ....

3. ....

This entry form must be post-marked by January 31 (Confirmations of the first 60 teams' entry will be sent shortly thereafter. Please call 753–2385 for any last-minute changes.

Oratory

1. ....

2. ....

3. ....

Address all communications to:
Steve Hunt or John Walker,
Tournament Directors,
Department of Speech,
University of Denver
Denver, Colorado 80210

Oral Interpretation

1. ....

2. ....

3. ....

SCHOOL ....

ADDRESS ....

COACH ....

JUDGE ....

SCHOOL TELEPHONE NO. ....

HOME TELEPHONE NO. ....

The next set of management tasks involves the jobs that must be completed to guarantee the successful operation of the tournament. The first task is building a *tournament staff* that will be responsible for general assignments. The *facilities of the tournament* must be arranged for, so that the director is assured of the rooms, lounges, and large meeting places that will be required. Also, a staff of *timekeepers* and *judges* must be obtained and steps taken to ensure that they meet the obligations they were assigned in advance of the tournament. The arrangements for *scheduling the competition* must be efficient and accurate. In addition, the *results of the tournament* must be tabulated accurately and as quickly as possible. Finally, the contest director must arrange for all of the *materials* that are necessary for all of the tasks that are involved in the administration and operation of the tournament.

When the tournament is over, the director must *announce the results* in a very detailed way, so that each contestant can tell how he fared in relation to the others, and then he must *publicize the results* of the tournament through the local news media so that the community at large will know who the winners were.

Now that the managerial tasks that face the tournament manager have been specified, we will consider the methods that have been successfully used to complete these tasks. The master notebook is essential for successful tournament direction.

THE MASTER NOTEBOOK

The master notebook system is used simply to ensure that all of the necessary tasks will be completed, that coordination of the tasks will be as easy as possible, and that the materials vital for the management of the tournament will be accessible. The notebook contains major headings for every important task, and, as the tasks are completed, entries or notations can be made in the notebook for reference in finishing subsequent duties. A new notebook should be prepared for each tournament, so that the director has a complete record of every tournament he manages. He can use the old notebooks to refresh his memory and to note mistakes that should be corrected or avoided in later tournaments.

The following organization is suggested for the basic master notebook. Because the details of every tournament or festival are different from all the others, the headings and subheadings will change to meet the circumstances.

1. SCHOOL REGISTRATION
   A. A complete list of schools, with code numbers identifying each school.
   B. School information, arrival times, motel arrangements, etc.

2. REGISTRATION FORMS
   (Here, all of the entry blanks for the visiting schools are filed. these may be checked for correction at the tournament registration before fees are assessed.)

3. EVENT REGISTRATION
   (All relevant information about each event is filed here. The following represents the subheadings for a typical tournament.)
   A. Debate
      (1) Tournament regulations
      (2) Divisions and entries, by contestant, in each division
      (3) Schedules ("Postings") for each round, showing who meets whom, who judges, and the room numbers.
   B. Extemporaneous Speaking
      (1) Tournament regulations
      (2) Postings for each round
      (3) Master list of extemporaneous speaking topics.
   C. Oratory
      (1) Tournament regulations
      (2) Postings for each round.
   D. Oral Interpretation
      (1) Tournament regulations
      (2) Postings for each round.

4. JUDGES
   (A complete list of the judges, with space to indicate the rounds for which they are available and where they have already been used.)

5. ROOMS
   (A complete list of the available rooms and the times at which they are available.)

6. ARRANGEMENTS FOR MEALS

7. RESULTS
   (Dittoed result sheets are placed here before the awards meetings.)

8. FINANCES

(A complete record of fees received and expenses incurred should be kept here.)

9. MISCELLANEOUS MATERIAL

A. The tournament announcement
B. Final schedule of events.

10. COMMENTS

(This can be one of the most useful sections, containing the tournament manager's comments and observations. This section also records mistakes and problems so that they can be avoided or handled better in the future.)

The following chapters will consider the best methods for fulfilling the essential management tasks—how to develop the material to place under the headings and subheadings in the master notebook.

CHAPTER 3

Preparations for the Event

THE DECISION TO HOLD A CONTEST

The decision to hold a forensic contest begins with the coach of the forensic squad. Many coaches are attracted to the idea of hosting a tournament because of the many advantages that accrue to the school that holds a contest. The host is able to enter a number of its students at little expense. The host school also gets a chance to reciprocate professionally for the tournaments it has attended. A well-run tournament, moreover, enhances the respect that others hold for the host school. Finally, by offering a tournament, the forensic coach is able to run a contest the way he thinks such a contest should be run and to schedule the events he thinks are most important.

Perhaps the major advantage in hosting a tournament is the educational development and managerial experience that is available to many students from the host school. Each student taking a specific responsibility for the tournament can learn responsibility, tact in dealing with others, skill in the particular task, and the value of dependability. Other areas of transfer may be in learning the importance of being accurate, punctual, and in the urgency of double and triple checking. The students involved in keeping time have the opportunity to see good and bad communication habits, hear skilled critics give various viewpoints on speech and the debate topic, and, of course, learn considerably about the subject matter.

More goes into the decision to host a contest, however, than the forensic teacher's desire or willingness to do so. Permission and approval must first be obtained from the administration of the school, and the immediate and major considerations for large tournaments are time, space, and the availability of proper facilities. For example, more rooms are needed for debate than for any other event: one room is required for every two debate teams entered. An assembly room is needed, a preparation room for extemporaneous speaking, a tabulations room, a coaches' room, and an adequate central area for handling the postings of events and for balloting.

If a school does not have adequate facilities or the facilities are not available, it is wise to decide not to host a contest or to hold events in conjunction with a nearby school. Many two-school tournaments are now developing.

The tournament manager also should verify the availability of adequate accommodations in hotels and motels for contestants from distant cities. The tournament director will generally find that hotel and motel managers wish to be helpful and work with him. For instance, the 1969 Glass City National Holiday Tournament in Toledo, Ohio found a major motel near the university willing to reserve units for up to two hundred people at special reduced rates. When this is possible, the tournament manager is well advised to directly handle reservations. An enclosed form with the entry blank such as below is adequate. A speech tournament once was held at the same time as a major Kiwanis convention and the visitors were forced to sleep in their cars. It is not hard to imagine how this affected their performance the next day.

HOTEL REGISTRATION FORM

School..

Moderator..

Please reserve rooms for the following:

Single Room $8 per night   Which nights?

1.   ....

2.   ....

Twin Room $5.50 per person per night   Which nights?

1.   ...., ...

2.   ...., ...

3.   ...., ...

Four in a room $4 per person per night

1.   ....

      ....

      ....

      ....

Five or six in a room $2 additional per person per night.
Payment will be made directly to the motel at check-out.

If all of the necessary facilities are available, the prospective tournament director is in a position to decide the kind of contest he wishes to offer and the time of year he should host it—provided he has the consent of the administration.

The administration in reality need do more than consent for an effective tournament to be developed. Strong and active support is necessary. Without such concern and feeling, a tournament is on dubious ground. Many items, in addition to good will, are contingent on administrative backing. Some simple illustrations are found in the areas of food service, custodial assistance, room availability, public relations, and general community wide interest.

A note might be added here about parent organizations. Many high school programs find that such groups are invaluable for serving food, helping with the tournament, judging, providing liaison with the area, and raising money for the program. High schools as far apart geographically as Texas, Florida, Missouri and Ohio have such active groups of parents raising up to thousands of dollars for the forensic program and aiding with the administration of tournaments.

Such groups may be mobilized by finding one, two, or three key individuals, calling an open meeting of all parents, electing officers, and establishing a planning committee.

THE NATURE OF THE CONTEST

As was mentioned earlier, there are three major reasons for attending a tournament. Contestants come for experience in forensics, for the educational benefits of interscholastic or intercollegiate tournament experience, and for the excitement of the competition. All three of these elements undoubtedly come into play in every forensic contest; however, a tournament can be structured so that one or another element is emphasized.

If the contest director wishes to provide maximal competitive emphasis, he should offer an elimination tournament in which the contestants go through several preliminary rounds, followed by, say, quarter-finals, semi-finals, and a final round to decide which contestant or team is the best. If he wishes, a comparative balance of the various elements, he should probably stage a "best-record" tournament; a winner is chosen but no elimination rounds are held. If he wishes to maximize the educational potential of the forensic situation, he can offer a festival in which only quality awards are given—in which a great deal of emphasis is placed on critiques from judges. A practice tournament also can place heavy emphasis on the educational and experience elements and still provide a good measure of competition. By offering a variety of divisions and events, the contest manager can emphasize different purposes and goals in different divisions, providing something for everybody.

Except for championship contests the time of year is not a crucial factor, but it is obvious, as was pointed out in Chapter 1, that some times are more appropriate than others for particular types of tournaments. Generally, the less competitive its emphasis, the earlier in the forensic season the contest should be. It is best to hold the more competitive tournaments later in the forensic season, when teams and contestants are reaching their peaks in competitive ability.

THE TOURNAMENT ANNOUNCEMENT

Most experienced tournament directors announce their tournament in two phases. First, they send a preliminary announcement of tournament dates and events. This serves as a planning guide for other forensic teachers. Then they send a complete announcement, about two months before the tournament. A sample preliminary announcement follows.

Preliminary Announcement

The Thirty-fifth Annual Rocky Mountain High School Forensic Tournament will be held at the University of Denver on February 20 and 21, 1970. If you are interested in participating in this tournament, please reserve this date. You will receive a more complete announcement in mid-December.

Once again, this will be an invitational tournament and you will be asked to submit an application for a bid to participate. Events will again include debate, oratory, extemporaneous speaking, and oral interpretation.

This announcement should be sent as early in the school year as possible—September is best; if any regional master calendars are available they should be checked and listed with. Schools planning major events should list with NFL, their state association, *Issues*, and their own area coaches.

Such an announcement serves as formal notification to the schools that will be invited to participate. Many tournament directors include a return postcard on which the invited schools can indicate their interest and intentions. Such information is very helpful when it

comes time to order supplies and confirm the facilities for the contest.
About two months prior to the date of the tournament is the best
time to prepare the final announcement, which must be as complete
and concise as possible. The decision to attend a tournament often
depends on a seemingly minor detail that is a major concern of a
coach. Incomplete information, moreover, often forms the basis for
problems that develop during a tournament.

Because of the unique nature of many tournaments it is impossible
to provide an outline for the tournament announcement that would
be practical in all situations; however, the following is a general
guide for the formulation of this type of letter.

1. Type and name of the contest.
2. Headquarters location and time of tournament registration.
3. Events that will be scheduled and a clear statement of divisions,
   such as men's, women's, upper, lower, novice, etc. Each should
   be carefully defined.
4. A definite indication of the time the tournament will conclude.

Debate

(*a*) Precise wording of the topic

(*b*) Number of persons on a team (if there are men's and women's
divisions, it is customary for mixed teams to be in the men's
division)

(*c*) Style of debate and time limitation

(*d*) Number of rounds and an explanation of the system that
will be used for determining winners

Discussion

(*a*) The topic

(*b*) Procedure and type of contest

(*c*) The method of evaluation, in detail

(*d*) A sample agenda

The discussion topic, "What should be the role of the university
in American society?" will be divided into sub-topics each round.
ROUND I—"What should be the nature of a liberal education
in the 1970's?"

The focus should be on the goals of a liberal education—what
it means to be educated liberally—and therefore, what should
be the purposes of higher education today?

Each group will assume that they have been asked to prepare a brief statement (in writing) on the nature of a liberal education. ROUND II—"In what respects are universities failing to accomplish their proper functions?"

This is a problem-analysis phase—the group will discuss shortcomings of universities and it will give consideration to the causes of the shortcomings. It will not attempt to propose solutions in this round. Rather, it will focus on those aspects of universities which might need to be changed, which ought to be areas of concern.

ROUND III—"What changes should be made in universities to enable them to fulfill their proper functions more effectively?"

This is a solution phase—here the group will try to agree on changes in curricula, teaching methods, public service policies, etc., of colleges and universities. Each participant should be prepared to advocate one or more specific changes; the group will discuss which of the proposed changes are significant enough to warrant priority.

Extemporaneous Speaking

(a) General area from which the topics will be drawn and means of obtaining topics
(b) Procedure for choosing topic and the time that will be allowed for preparation
(c) Time limits for the speeches
(d) Limitations on the use of notes
(e) Method of evaluation
(f) A typical topic will be: What further steps should the present Nixon Administration take to combat inflation?

Impromptu Speaking

(a) General area from which the topics will be drawn and means by which topics are obtained
(b) Time limits for the speeches
(c) Method of evaluation

Oratory or Persuasive Speaking

(a) Manuscript requirements. If manuscripts must be turned in at registration, this must be clearly stated
(b) Amount of quoted material that can be used (usually 10%)
(c) Time limits for the speeches

(*d*) Method of evaluation

Interpretive Events

(*a*) Type of reading, from memory or manuscript
(*b*) Type of literature acceptable (often from a specific list of authors or designated eras)
(*c*) Admonitions on acting and interpretation (a definition of interpretation is helpful)
(*d*) Time limits for presentations
(*e*) Method of evaluation

4. Schedule for all events, and time and place of registration for the tournament

5. Rules, time limitations, and number of participants per event per school

6. Eligibility rules
   (*a*) Qualifications for the various divisions
   (*b*) Number of events a student may enter

7. Fees
   (*a*) Charge per student for entry in individual events
   (*b*) Charges for debate teams
   (*c*) Charges for judging fees
       (1) Indicate whether a judge or judges must be furnished by participating schools
       (2) Indicate the credit (fee remission) that will be given for judges brought by the schools
       (3) Charges and necessary arrangements for judges to be furnished by the host school
   (*d*) Special charges
       (1) Banquet fees
       (2) Late registration fees

8. Entry blank (the one- or two-page entry blank should ask for *all* of the information the manager will need for setting up the tournament)
   (*a*) Name of each person in each event and division
   (*b*) Names of the members of the debate teams in each division
   (*c*) Names of judges to be provided
   (*d*) Name, address, office and home telephone numbers of each visiting school's director of forensics

Wherever possible, competent students should be recruited to perform appropriate tasks.

(*e*) Name of visiting school

(*f*) Compilation of fees

(see page 26 for illustration)

9. Awards: by types and events, and explanation of point system for making awards

10. Deadline for return of entries

11. Parking information and general regulations, such as school policy on smoking, etc.

12. List of on-campus and off-campus lodging and eating facilities, including rates where possible

A sample of the form that can be used for the tournament announcement can be found in the sample master notebook in the Appendix and invitations and announcements received from other schools also can serve as guides in the preparation of this notification. After the follow-up announcement has been mailed, the contest manager is ready to turn to the task of preparing for the specific jobs that must be done before the tournament. The first step is arranging for the tournament's staff.

THE TOURNAMENT STAFF

Deciding who should be on the tournament staff and the areas they should be responsible for is one of the most important decisions and phases in tournament management. Unless the tournament director has had considerable experience, it is difficult to know what committees are necessary and who should be assigned to the various committee posts. It is poor management, of course, to have committees that are not needed or tasks that should be performed by committees that have not been appointed.

It is best to be very cautious in appointing committees and committee members, although there are tasks that probably will warrant committee assignments. For example, rooms and facilities, event scheduling and direction, timekeeping, judging, tabulations, and hosting the tournament must be considered in the early stages of planning.

The person or committee in charge of rooms and facilities should get written permission for their use at the times they will be needed. This information is important for the persons who will schedule the events, for they, in turn, must keep the room committee informed of their needs as they plan their operations. It is also important that the facilities be "nailed down" well ahead of time, to guarantee that adequate space will be available on tournament day. The committee must check on whether or not each room is unlocked and open before each round.

The committee for event scheduling and direction is one of the two most important committees in the tournament structure. The most experienced and responsible students should be assigned to this task. The scheduling committee sets up the pairings for all debate rounds and schedules the competition in the individual events. The details of their job will be discussed in Chapter 4.

Timekeepers are usually secured from the student body of the host school, and often they are students who are enrolled in speech classes. The speech teacher may require that they "volunteer" this service or he may give extra credit to those who do. Typically, the timekeeper also serves as the chairman. He has the primary responsibility for seeing that the judges and all of the contestants assigned to his event (or section of the event) are ready to start at the scheduled time. It is best to have the ballot carried from headquarters to the room and the completed ballot returned to the tabulation room by him.

The committee to secure judges must work closely with the tournament manager so that only the best-qualified judges are obtained to supplement those from the visiting schools. The judges should have extensive debate and judging experience and should be college graduates. The most important consideration is that they know the rules of forensics that apply to the criticism of the forensic events that are being offered. Unqualified judges—the police chief or a prominent attorney—though well intentioned, can do much more harm than good when they apply their subjective criteria to the work of students who have prepared to perform in front of an experienced critic. Certainly, the basketball or football team would not consider hiring the police chief or a clergyman to referee a game unless they were very sure that they were fully qualified to officiate.

Experience with guest judges indicates a number of steps that should be taken to assure their meeting their obligations on tournament day. Prospective judges should be asked, at least a month before the contest, if they will assist at the tournament. Then they should be sent a letter of confirmation, and finally a reminder note or call just before the tournament. Of course, the best way to get willing and qualified judges is to pay them adequately for their services. Entry fees usually can be adjusted so that extra critics can be hired, and judging fees can be assessed to provide judges that schools fail to bring to the contest.

The tabulations committee is another important committee in the tournament or festival organization. The best-run tournament can easily be discredited if the results are tabulated incorrectly or too slowly. Few things are as embarrassing to a contest manager as giving an award to the wrong person or making hundreds of contestants wait past the announced time for the results to be announced.

The operational details of the tabulations committee will be outlined in Chapter 4, but at this point it can be said that responsible students must be assigned to this committee. Three or four persons who can be trusted to work quickly and harmoniously should be selected. They must be willing to admit the possibility that they will make mistakes in tabulations and therefore be willing to check and double check their calculations. The director should personally check the final result sheet.

The committee for hosting the tournament can be made up of persons whose characteristics disqualify them for exacting assignments. This is the place for the extroverted public-relations-type student, for this committee is responsible for greeting the guests and making their stay at the tournament as enjoyable as possible. Its duties include registration work, distributing and collecting ballots, helping people find housing, helping contestants locate their assigned rooms, and generally providing a "positive atmosphere" for the tournament. It is wise to select students for this committee who will remain calm and cordial under pressure. If panic sweeps through the tabulations room, the hosting committee should make it appear that everything is under control and that the tournament is running smoothly, as planned.

FACILITIES AND MATERIALS

Although a list of required facilities was given at the beginning of this chapter, several related items also must be noted. After the rooms for the competition, the assembly room, and so forth have been arranged, it is necessary to make sure that they are adequately furnished and designated. All of the rooms should have a podium or speaker's stand and enough chairs and tables for the contestants and judges. The rooms should be clearly marked, so that the posting designations are clear and the rooms are easy to locate. Printed cards can signify rooms that have been reserved for the contest, and that latecomers should not enter.

If the tournament or festival is large and adequate facilities are a problem, room and building committees should be assigned by the facilities committee. The building chairman can see that rooms are open and that the rounds are started on time. Many contest managers have the building chairman collect ballots and post schedules so that contestants and judges do not have to return to the tournament headquarters between rounds to learn where they should go next (perhaps back to the room they just came from).

The materials for a tournament should be obtained early, and usually can be purchased at a discount if they are bought early enough. A list of the necessary equipment and supplies typically includes the following items.

Equipment

Typewriters	Headquarters telephone
Duplicating machines	Bulletin boards
Adding machine or calculator	Cash box

Supplies

Several reams of duplicating paper	Carbon paper
Duplicating masters	Several large poster boards for tabulating results
11″ × 14″ envelopes for registration materials and results	Envelopes for ballots
Ballots (AFA form C is frequently used)	Time cards
A receipt book	Instruction sheets for judges and timekeepers
Name tags	Campus maps
Certificates and tropies	
	Secretarial supplies: pencils, pens felt-tip pens, stapler and staples, tape, thumbtacks, paper clips, erasers, and yardsticks and rulers

Trophies, of course, are a substantial expense for a contest; however, if they are ordered far in advance, discounts can be obtained. The tournament manager or one of his assistants should canvass several trophy companies, check the kinds of trophies that are available, and seek to get a discount if the tournament agrees to return year after year with a trophy order. If his budget is skimpy, the tournament manager can buy the least expensive trophies, such as the traditional loving cup, and can eliminate unnecessary engraving. Occasionally a great deal of money can be saved on discontinued trophy models. The most expensive prizes will almost always be the newest and most popular styles of trophies.

Ballots for the critics of the various events are a special problem for contest managers, Many experienced directors order their ballots from the American Forensic Association, which offers several types of debate ballots with selfcarbon paper that yields three copies of the ballots. However, it is not unusual for a tournament director to design his own ballots to fit the special needs of his tournament. The set of ballots shown below was designed by Alan G. Price of the staff of the University of Denver. They have proved highly useful and are very easy and inexpensive to reproduce. This type of ballot has a comment sheet for each team or contestant, in addition to a ballot summary sheet. The individual sheets can be given to the contestants after the tournament and the summary sheets can be kept in the tournament files for reference.

DEBATE BALLOT

Decision to the (Aff.) (Neg.) team from school........................ Affirmative: ....

	Sup.	Exc.	Good	Fair	Poor	
1st Aff.	10 9	8 7	6 5	4 3	2 1	Negative: ....
2nd Aff.	10 9	8 7	6 5	4 3	2 1	Round: 1 2 3 4 5 6 F

	Sup.	Exc.	Good	Fair	Poor	
1st Neg.	10 9	8 7	6 5	4 3	2 1	Room: ....
2nd Neg.	10 9	8 7	6 5	4 3	2 1	Judge: ....

Signed:..

School:..

DEBATE BALLOT

	Sup.	Exc.	Good	Fair	Poor
1st (Aff. or Neg.)............	10 9	8 7	6 5	5 4	2 1
2nd (Aff. or Neg.)...........	10 9	8 7	6 5	4 3	2 1

Affirmative: ....

Negative:...................................

Decision to the .... team from...

Reason for the decision:

Round: 1 2 3 4 5 6 F

Room:..

Judge: ....

FACTORS CONSIDERED:

Analysis:

Organization:

Evidence:

Refutation:

Delivery:

OTHER COMMENTS:

Signed:...

School:...

INDIVIDUAL EVENTS BALLOT

This is your official ballot. Please circle the appropriate ratings and rankings for each contestant below. Give no ties for 1st, 2nd or 3rd rankings; give no rankings below 4th. Ties may be given on ratings.

Event: E   O   I

Round: 1   2   3   F

Room:...............................

Judge:...............................

1. .... Rank: *1st* *2nd* *3rd* *4th*
Rating: 10   9 8   7 6   5 4   3   2   1

2. .... Rank: *1st* *2nd* *3rd* *4th*
Rating: 10   9 8   7 6   5 4   3   2   1

3. .... Rank: *1st* *2nd* *3rd* *4th*
Rating: 10   9 8   7 6   5 4   3   2   1

4. .... Rank: *1st* *2nd* *3rd* *4th*
Rating: 10   9 8   7 6   5 4   3   2   1

5. .... Rank: *1st* *2nd* *3rd* *4th*
Rating: 10   9 8   7 6   5 4   3   2   1

6. .... Rank: *1st* *2nd* *3rd* *4th*
Rating: 10   9 8   7 6   5 4   3   2   1

7. .... Rank: *1st* *2nd* *3rd* *4th*
Rating: 10   9 8   7 6   5 4   3   2   1

Signed:...............................

School:...............................

ORAL INTERPRETATION OF DRAMATIC LITERATURE

CRITIQUE FOR ....
(*Please complete*)

Indicate a score for each quality, using the following scale: 5, outstanding; 4, excellent; 3, good; 2, fair; 1, poor. OR indicate a + for above average, 0 for average, and − for needs improvement. If you use the numbers, this sheet may aid you in the ranking of contestants. In any case, it will be given to the contestant as a critique sheet.

     I. *Selection*
        1. Comprehension of material   ....
        2. Interpretation of
             emotional content   ....
             logical content   ....

    II. *Intensity of feeling*
        1. Expression of mood   ....
        2. Display of vigor, life, emphasis,
           force, humanness, or warmth   ....

   III. *Voice*
        1. Variety   ....
        2. Control   ....
        3. Quality   ....
        4. Pronunciation   ....
        5. Articulation   ....

   IV. *Time*
        Variety   ....
        Effective use of rate   ....

    V. *Physical Expression*
        1. Posture   ....
        2. Gestures   ....
        3. Correlation of selection and
           physical expression   ....
        4. Facial Expression   ....

NUMBER OF CONTESTANT..
ROUND NUMBER..
JUDGE..

COMMENTS:

4

ORIGINAL ORATORY

CRITIQUE FOR ....
(Please complete)

Indicate a score for each quality, using the following scale: 5, outstanding; 4, excellent; 3, good; 2, fair; 1, poor. OR, indicate a + for above average, 0 for average, and − for needs improvement. If you use the numbers, this sheet may aid you in the ranking of contestants. In any case, it will be given to the contestant as a critique sheet.

I. *Selection*
   1. Comprehension of material ....
   2. Interpretation of
       emotional content ....
       logical content ....

II. *Intensity of feeling*
   1. Expression of mood ....
   2. Display of vigor, life, emphasis,
       force, humanness, or warmth ....

III. *Voice*
   1. Variety ....
   2. Control ....
   3. Quality ....
   4. Pronunciation ....
   5. Articulation ....

IV. *Time*
   Variety ....
   Effective use of rate ....

V. *Physical Expression*
   1. Posture ....
   2. Gestures ....
   3. Correlation of selection
       and physical expression ....
   4. Facial Expression ....

NUMBER OF CONTESTANT...
ROUND NUMBER...
JUDGE.....................................

COMMENTS:

EXTEMPORANEOUS SPEAKING

CRITIQUE FOR ....
(Please complete)

Indicate a score for each quality, using the following scale: 5, outstanding; 4, excellent; 3, good; 2, fair; 1, poor. OR indicate a + for above average, 0 for average, and − for needs improvement. If you use the numbers, this sheet may aid you in the ranking of contestants. In any case, it will be given to the contestant as a critique sheet.

I. *Content*
   1. Understanding   ....
   2. Analysis   ....
   3. Knowledge   ....
   4. Organization   ....

II. *Voice*
   1. Variety   ....
   2. Control   ....
   3. Quality   ....
   4. Pronunciation   ....
   5. Articulation   ....

III. *Time*
   1. Variety   ....
   2. Effective use of rate   ....

IV. *Physical Expression*
   1. Posture   ....
   2. Gestures   ....
   3. Correlation of selection and
      physical expression   ....
   4. Facial Expression   ....

NUMBER OF CONTESTANT...
ROUND NUMBER...
JUDGE...

COMMENTS:

DISCUSSION EVALUATION FORM

Your Name...

Name of Participant...

Rating scale: Using the following plan of rating, assign a numerical rating for each of the factors used, and write comments where appropriate.

1	2	3	4	5
Poor	Fair	Average	Good	Excellent

	Rating	Reason for Rating
1. Non-verbal communication	....	
2. Voice and articulation	....	
3. Information-giving	....	
4. Clarification-giving	....	
5. Solution-giving	....	
6. Solution-evaluating	....	
7. Organization of contributions	....	
8. Quality of evidence	....	
9. Quality of reasoning	....	
10. Procedural helper	....	
11. "Tie-in" contributions	....	
12. Influence exerted	....	
13. Group unity builder	....	

OVERALL RATING:

Whatever form of ballot is used, there are important features it must have. Its criteria must be clear to the judge. It must be relatively easy to fill out. Its design must minimize the possibility of mistakes. And it should have room for individual comments, so that each contestant can have a written "feedback" on every performance.

CHAPTER 4

Tournament Direction

Although adequate preparation is the key to efficient contest management, many tasks simply cannot be done far in advance of tournament day. On-the-spot physical arrangements must be made at the last minute, because it's not until then that the tournament staff has access to the facilities it has reserved. Events cannot be scheduled until a day or two before the contest because of many last-minute changes in registration and other problems.

Even after a so-called "final" scheduling, the director must be prepared for last minute "drops" that will completely disrupt the schedule. The only good alternative is to have a series of schedules, allowing for several drops, on stencil, ready for duplication that can be prepared at the end of registration. It is too late to actually prepare at that point, but if schedules are ready, the correct one can be chosen and duplicated, i.e. If the final count shows twenty-two teams, have schedules for fifteen to twenty-two teams ready to run off.

After the contestants arrive, the tournament staff must register them, indicate their speaking and judging schedules, and tabulate the results of their competitive efforts; last of all, before the contest is officially over, the awards have to be given.

This chapter deals solely with the tasks that must be done immediately before and during the contest. It tries to present practical suggestions for getting these jobs done as efficiently as possible.

PHYSICAL ARRANGEMENTS FOR CONTEST OPERATION

The physical arrangements for the *management* of the tournament should include (1) a registration center, (2) a tabulation room, (3) a meeting room for contestants, (4) a standby room for judges, (5) a desk for the assignment of judges, (6) a place for posting the schedules for rounds and other announcements, and (7) a desk for timekeepers.

The registration center (the first area to be put to use) in its simplest form consists of two or three long tables that are joined end to end. Signs attached to the tables indicate the various stages of registration (see Figure A). The first stage usually is the checking station where a member of the tournament staff goes over the entry blanks with the schools' coaches to see that the original entries are correct. Then comes the financial station, where the visiting coaches pay their fees. (It is becoming a practice of many tournaments to have fees paid with the registration form.) At the next station, coaches should be able to pick up a packet of materials that are relevant to the tournament. It is also a good idea to establish an information station at the registration desk, where contestants and coaches can ask questions about the city or the tournament. This area should be out of the general registration traffic flow, such as to the rear or far side.

FIGURE A

REGISTRATION CENTER

(1)	(2)	(3)	(4)
CHECKING STATION	FINANCIAL STATION	TOURNAMENT MATERIALS AND INFORMATION	INFORMATION CENTER

When the registration period ends, many contest managers use the tables as desks for running the tournament. The tables can now be relabeled to include a table that will be used by the person in charge of assigning judges and a table that will be used for assigning timekeepers. The judges' ballots, when completed, are returned to the judges' table and the timekeepers' return the time cards to the timekeepers' table. (See Figure B.) Bulletin boards can be placed near these tables so that contestants and judges can conveniently check schedules and announcements.

FIGURE B

TOURNAMENT CENTER (CONVERTED FROM REGISTRATION CENTER)

(1)	(2)	(3)	(4)
JUDGES' TABLE (Ballots are picked up here)	TIMEKEEPERS' TABLE	EXTRA SCHEDULES AND ASSIGNMENTS	INFORMATION

The judges' standby room can be one of the most useful or "strategic" tournament facilities. The tournament director should provide a room in which judges can lounge, and so attractive that they will naturally gravitate to it. Coffee and doughnuts should be provided along with comfortable chairs and smoking facilities. Such a facility is an important asset in attracting competent judges.

Since it is imperative to be able to find judges when they are needed, a means needs to be found to either keep them in this room or know where they are. The staff member in charge of judges should have a master list showing where each judge should be each hour. He should check the completed rounds off when the judge returns. Timekeepers *may be* instructed to endeavor to get the judge to return. One added sidelight that can be very helpful is a television section of the lounge. This is especially true when sports events are on the screen. Another feature that will help is to have daily papers and periodical reading material available in another section of the lounge. If judges feel it necessary to leave, the staff member should note where that judge will be and how long.

MASTER CHART

	9:00 a.m.	10:15 a.m.	11:30 a.m.	1:00 p.m.	2:15 p.m.
Howard Sharfe	Debate 101 SM	Extemp ES 210	Debate 210 UH	Free	Oratory ES 101

The tabulations room has rather simple requirements. It should be removed from the flow of tournament traffic but fairly close to the judges' table, where ballots are turned in. It should have several large tables and enough room for typewriters and duplicating equipment. Naturally, tabulations rooms should be labeled "off limits" to all who are not immediately concerned with tabulating results. The rationale for this is not so much the question of secrecy that many assume, but the mere factor that excess noise and traffic will be likely to predispose the tabulations crew to errors.

The tabulations room should have typewriters, duplicating machines, adequate paper, charts, pens, markers, pencils, erasers, tables, and chairs.

The contestants' meeting room should be the largest room the tournament manager has at his disposal. Typically, a gymnasium or auditorium can serve as the meeting room, lounging area for contestants, the place for posting tournament announcements, and the place for drawing topics for extemporaneous speaking.

SCHEDULING TOURNAMENT EVENTS

Scheduling is one of the most critical periods in the life of a contest, and the making of the "perfect" tournament. The scheduling chairman must bring the judges and contestants together in such a way that no contestants compete with each other more than once, and a judge does not hear his own contestants at all or an individual contestant more than once.

When it is at all possible, a judge should not hear a team on the

DIAGRAM FOR TABULATIONS ROOM LAYOUT

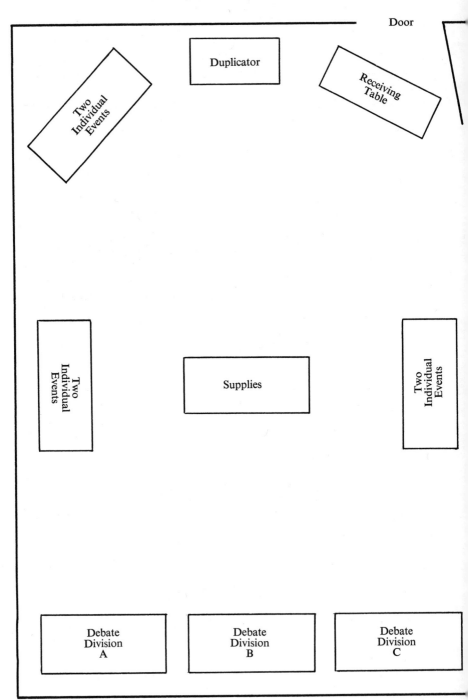

affirmative that his team will debate later in the tournament, especially where they would not debate for several rounds or the next day. Here again the issue is not so much secrecy as that of promoting good feelings among coaches and debaters. If this task is completed properly, the tournament or festival will practically run itself.

The model for scheduling that is presented later in this chapter represents the form that is used in the vast majority of tournaments and festivals. Because of the large number of participants in each contest, the director can seldom resort to the scheduling techniques that often are used in other types of competitions. Such methods as the round-robin elimination system are used only in a handful of tournaments because they are not practical for events that involve, say, a hundred contestants who compete in a one- or two-day contest.

DEBATE. Debate should be scheduled a day or two before the contest begins, by which time the various coaches should have notified the director of changes in their registration. If teams drop out at the last minute, tournament directors may substitute one of their own teams or provide for a default.

As indicated in the opening of this chapter, this is not the ideal answer since it defeats the educational values of the tournament by reducing the competitive rounds for the teams involved in forfeits; but if the manager does not have alternative schedules ready, he may forfeit round one and reorganize the schedule for future rounds.

Four man debate should be scheduled on a schematic similar to one of the two types included in these examples of schedules for tournaments ranging from eight to twenty teams.

The following pages will represent a variety of practices in use in various parts of the country. Often three round tournaments are held for a small number of entries. Four, five and even six round events are becoming common.

Numbers are assigned by various practices. They may be pre-set by the tournament staff or they may be selected at random by a team representative upon arrival.

On the first schedule you will notice at the top of each judge column that the system is started with judge 5, jump 3 and then drop back to two. Notice on the schedules from ten teams through nineteen the starting judge number is rotated in the same manner, jump three, drop back to three and then two for four rounds of competition. In the final example of twenty teams in four man debate, the system is somewhat different. We start with judge seven then jump three, drop back five, then two, and then for round five jump to the final number, i.e. twenty.

Debate Schedules

The following schedule will work for eight teams debating a four-man, non-switch sides format.

	ROUND I			ROUND II			ROUND III		
Aff.	Neg.	Judge	Aff.	Neg.	Judge	Aff.	Neg.	Judge	Room
1	2	5	1	3	8	1	4	2	
2	3	6	2	4	1	2	5	3	
3	4	7	3	5	2	3	6	4	
4	5	8	4	6	3	4	7	5	
5	6	1	5	7	4	5	8	6	
6	7	2	6	8	5	6	1	7	
7	8	3	7	1	6	7	2	8	
8	1	4	8	2	7	8	3	1	

The following schedule can be used as a means for structuring a ten team four-man, non-switch sides tournament.

	ROUND I			ROUND II			ROUND III			ROUND IV		
Aff.	Neg.	Judge	Aff.	Neg.	Judge	Aff.	Neg.	Judge	Aff.	Neg.	Judge	Room
1	2	6	1	3	9	1	4	3	1	5	2	
2	3	7	2	4	10	2	5	4	2	6	3	
3	4	8	3	5	1	3	6	5	3	7	4	
4	5	9	4	6	2	4	7	6	4	8	5	
5	6	10	5	7	3	5	8	7	5	9	6	
6	7	1	6	8	4	6	9	8	6	10	7	
7	8	2	7	9	5	7	10	9	7	1	8	
8	9	3	8	10	6	8	1	10	8	2	9	
9	10	4	9	1	7	9	2	1	9	3	10	
10	1	5	10	2	8	10	3	2	10	4	1	

Another form used in posting schedules is by only listing affirmatives once as in the following examples.

ELEVEN TEAM SCHEDULE

	ROUND I		ROUND II		ROUND III		ROUND IV		
Aff.	Neg.	Judge	Neg.	Judge	Neg.	Judge	Neg.	Judge	Room
1	2	7	3	10	4	3	5	2	
2	3	8	4	11	5	4	6	3	
3	4	9	5	1	6	5	7	4	
4	5	10	6	2	7	6	8	5	
5	6	11	7	3	8	7	9	6	
6	7	1	8	4	9	8	10	7	
7	8	2	9	5	10	9	11	8	
8	9	3	10	6	11	10	1	9	
9	10	4	11	7	1	11	2	10	
10	11	5	1	8	2	1	3	11	
11	1	6	2	9	3	2	4	1	

TWELVE TEAM SCHEDULE

1	2	8	3	11	4	3	5	2	
2	3	9	4	12	5	4	6	3	
3	4	10	5	1	6	5	7	4	
4	5	11	6	2	7	6	8	5	
5	6	12	7	3	8	7	9	6	
6	7	1	8	4	9	8	10	7	
7	8	2	9	5	10	9	11	8	
8	9	3	10	6	11	10	12	9	
9	10	4	11	7	12	11	1	10	
10	11	5	12	8	1	12	2	11	
11	12	6	1	9	2	1	3	12	
12	1	7	2	10	3	2	4	1	

59

THIRTEEN TEAM SCHEDULE

	ROUND I		ROUND II		ROUND III		ROUND IV		
Aff.	Neg.	Judge	Neg.	Judge	Neg.	Judge	Neg.	Judge	Room
1	2	9	3	12	4	3	5	2	
2	3	10	4	13	5	4	6	3	
3	4	11	5	1	6	5	7	4	
4	5	12	6	2	7	6	8	5	
5	6	13	7	3	8	7	9	6	
6	7	1	8	4	9	8	10	7	
7	8	2	9	5	10	9	11	8	
8	9	3	10	6	11	10	12	9	
9	10	4	11	7	12	11	13	10	
10	11	5	12	8	13	12	1	11	
11	12	6	13	9	1	13	2	12	
12	13	7	1	10	2	1	3	13	
13	1	8	2	11	3	2	4	1	

FOURTEEN TEAM SCHEDULE

	ROUND I		ROUND II		ROUND III		ROUND IV		
Aff.	Neg.	Judge	Neg.	Judge	Neg.	Judge	Neg.	Judge	Room
1	2	10	3	13	4	3	5	2	
2	3	11	4	14	5	4	6	3	
3	4	12	5	1	6	5	7	4	
4	5	13	6	2	7	6	8	5	
5	6	14	7	3	8	7	9	6	
6	7	1	8	4	9	8	10	7	
7	8	2	9	5	10	9	11	8	
8	9	3	10	6	11	10	12	9	
9	10	4	11	7	12	11	13	10	
10	11	5	12	8	13	12	14	11	
11	12	6	13	9	14	13	1	12	
12	13	7	14	10	1	14	2	13	
13	14	8	1	11	2	1	3	14	
14	1	9	2	12	3	2	4	1	

FIFTEEN TEAM SCHEDULE

	ROUND I		ROUND II		ROUND III		ROUND IV		
Aff.	Neg.	Judge	Neg.	Judge	Neg.	Judge	Neg.	Judge	Room
1	2	11	3	14	4	3	5	2	
2	3	12	4	15	5	4	6	3	
3	4	13	5	1	6	5	7	4	
4	5	14	6	2	7	6	8	5	
5	6	15	7	3	8	7	9	6	
6	7	1	8	4	9	8	10	7	
7	8	2	9	5	10	9	11	8	
8	9	3	10	6	11	10	12	9	
9	10	4	11	7	12	11	13	10	
10	11	5	12	8	13	12	14	11	
11	12	6	13	9	14	13	15	12	
12	13	7	14	10	15	14	1	13	
13	14	8	15	11	1	15	2	14	
14	15	9	1	12	2	1	3	15	
15	1	10	2	13	3	2	4	1	

SIXTEEN TEAM SCHEDULE

	ROUND I		ROUND II		ROUND III		ROUND IV		
Aff.	Neg.	Judge	Neg.	Judge	Neg.	Judge	Neg.	Judge	Room
1	2	12	3	15	4	3	5	2	
2	3	13	4	16	5	4	6	3	
3	4	14	5	1	6	5	7	4	
4	5	15	6	2	7	6	8	5	
5	6	16	7	3	8	7	9	6	
6	7	1	8	4	9	8	10	7	
7	8	2	9	5	10	9	11	8	
8	9	3	10	6	11	10	12	9	
9	10	4	11	7	12	11	13	10	
10	11	5	12	8	13	12	14	11	
11	12	6	13	9	14	13	15	12	
12	13	7	14	10	15	14	16	13	
13	14	8	15	11	16	15	1	14	
14	15	9	16	12	1	16	2	15	
15	16	10	1	13	2	1	3	16	
16	1	11	2	14	3	2	4	1	

SEVENTEEN TEAM SCHEDULE

	ROUND I		ROUND II		ROUND III		ROUND IV		
Aff.	Neg.	Judge	Neg.	Judge	Neg.	Judge	Neg.	Judge	Room
1	2	13	3	16	4	3	5	2	
2	3	14	4	17	5	4	6	3	
3	4	15	5	1	6	5	7	4	
4	5	16	6	2	7	6	8	5	
5	6	17	7	3	8	7	9	6	
6	7	1	8	4	9	8	10	7	
7	8	2	9	5	10	9	11	8	
8	9	3	10	6	11	10	12	9	
9	10	4	11	7	12	11	13	10	
10	11	5	12	8	13	12	14	11	
11	12	6	13	9	14	13	15	12	
12	13	7	14	10	15	14	16	13	
13	14	8	15	11	16	15	17	14	
14	15	9	16	12	17	16	1	15	
15	16	10	17	13	1	17	2	16	
16	17	11	1	14	2	1	3	17	
17	1	12	2	15	3	2	4	1	

EIGHTEEN TEAM SCHEDULE

	ROUND I		ROUND II		ROUND III		ROUND IV		
Aff.	Neg.	Judge	Neg.	Judge	Neg.	Judge	Neg.	Judge	Room
1	2	14	3	17	4	3	5	2	
2	3	15	4	18	5	4	6	3	
3	4	16	5	1	6	5	7	4	
4	5	17	6	2	7	6	8	5	
5	6	18	7	3	8	7	9	6	
6	7	1	8	4	9	8	10	7	
7	8	2	9	5	10	9	11	8	
8	9	3	10	6	11	10	12	9	
9	10	4	11	7	12	11	13	10	
10	11	5	12	8	13	12	14	11	
11	12	6	13	9	14	13	15	12	
12	13	7	14	10	15	14	16	13	
13	14	8	15	11	16	15	17	14	
14	15	9	16	12	17	16	18	15	
15	16	10	17	13	18	17	1	16	
16	17	11	18	14	1	18	2	17	
17	18	12	1	15	2	1	3	18	
18	1	13	2	16	3	2	4	1	

NINETEEN TEAM SCHEDULE

Aff.	ROUND I Neg.	Judge	ROUND II Neg.	Judge	ROUND III Neg.	Judge	ROUND IV Neg.	Judge	Room
1	2	15	3	18	4	3	5	2	
2	3	16	4	19	5	4	6	3	
3	4	17	5	1	6	5	7	4	
4	5	18	6	2	7	6	8	5	
5	6	19	7	3	8	7	9	6	
6	7	1	8	4	9	8	10	7	
7	8	2	9	5	10	9	11	8	
8	9	3	10	6	11	10	12	9	
9	10	4	11	7	12	11	13	10	
10	11	5	12	8	13	12	14	11	
11	12	6	13	9	14	13	15	12	
12	13	7	14	10	15	14	16	13	
13	14	8	15	11	16	15	17	14	
14	15	9	16	12	17	16	18	15	
15	16	10	17	13	18	17	19	16	
16	17	11	18	14	19	18	1	17	
17	18	12	19	15	1	19	2	18	
18	19	13	1	16	2	1	3	19	
19	1	14	2	17	3	2	4	1	

The following schedule would work for twenty teams in a four-man, non-switch sides tournament. Notice the different schematic approach in this schedule.

ROUND I Aff.	Neg.	Judge	ROUND II Aff.	Neg.	Judge	ROUND III Aff.	Neg.	Judge	ROUND IV Aff.	Neg.	Judge	ROUND V Aff.	Neg.	Judge	Room
1	2	7	1	3	10	1	4	5	1	5	3	1	6	20	
2	3	8	2	4	11	2	5	6	2	6	4	2	7	1	
3	4	9	3	5	12	3	6	7	3	7	5	3	8	2	
4	5	10	4	6	13	4	7	8	4	8	6	4	9	3	
5	6	11	5	7	14	5	8	9	5	9	7	5	10	4	
6	7	12	6	8	15	6	9	10	6	10	8	6	11	5	
7	8	13	7	9	16	7	10	11	7	11	9	7	12	6	
8	9	14	8	10	17	8	11	12	8	12	10	8	13	7	
9	10	15	9	11	18	9	12	13	9	13	11	9	14	8	
10	11	16	10	12	19	10	13	14	10	14	12	10	15	9	
11	12	17	11	13	20	11	14	15	11	15	13	11	16	10	
12	13	18	12	14	1	12	15	16	12	16	14	12	17	11	
13	14	19	13	15	2	13	16	17	13	17	15	13	18	12	
14	15	20	14	16	3	14	17	18	14	18	16	14	19	13	
15	16	1	15	17	4	15	18	19	15	19	17	15	20	14	
16	17	2	16	18	5	16	19	20	16	20	18	16	1	15	
17	18	3	17	19	6	17	20	1	17	1	19	17	2	16	
18	19	4	18	20	7	18	1	2	18	2	20	18	3	17	
19	20	5	19	1	8	19	2	3	19	3	1	19	4	18	
20	1	6	20	2	9	20	3	4	20	4	2	20	5	19	

If one uses numbers alone, confusion can more easily occur. A tournament in Michigan that experimented with numbers only in the two-man switchside event found that a great deal of confusion resulted. Tournaments in the mid-South using the letter-number combination have been highly successful in avoiding this confusion.

Another possibility that needs to be considered is the switchsides two-man tournament. The best way of coding this is by letter and number. For example, if a school has two two-man teams—one would be coded A_1 and the other A_2. The following examples illustrate the scheduling process.

EXAMPLE

(Step 1)

Affirmative

A_1
A_2
B_1
B_2
C_1
D_1
D_2
E_1
F_1
F_2
G_1
H_1

Next the teams should be spaced so that the teams from the same schools are spaced far enough apart so that they will not meet the same school twice in whatever the number of rounds, i.e. If the tournament is four rounds they should be separated by five places.

(Step 2)

Affirmative	*Negative*
A_1	J_1
B_1	K_1
C_1	L_1
D_1	M_1
E_1	N_1
A_2	P_1
B_2	O_1
F_1	N_2
D_2	J_2
F_2	K_2
G_1	L_2
H_1	M_2

The next procedure would be to add the judges and rooms.

(Step 3)

ROUND I

Affirmative	Negative	Judge	Room
A_1	J_1	E	101
B_1	K_1	A	103
C_1	L_1	K	105
D_1	M_1	C	107
E_1	N_1	D	108
A_2	J_2	F	109
B_2	K_2	G	111
F_1	L_2	H	112
G_1	M_2	J	114
H_1	N_2	L	115
D_2	O_1	M	116
F_1	P_1	N	117

Standby O-P-B

The final step is to add rounds II, III, and IV. The columns are advanced or rotated and checked by the same system as for four man debate. As you note, these teams are spaced in such a manner as to allow for four rounds. If a fifth round were added, the teams would meet unless you allowed for one more slot by spacing six apart.

To schedule the next two rounds of debate it is necessary to advance or rotate the columns. The judges' column should be rotated one way and one of the debate columns—in this case the Round I Negative—should be rotated the other way.

The debate postings are now complete, except for checking for errors, and it is time to go back through the postings to make a list of the competing teams and the judges' assignments. The chart that is shown below is used by many contest directors.

The judge's assignments may be checked as follows in this example:

Judge 5—1–2	6–8	4–7	
Judge 6—2–3	7–1	5–8	
Judge 7—3–4	8–2	6–1	
Judge 8—4–5	1–3	7–2	
Judge 1—5–6	2–4	8–3	
Judge 2—6–7	3–5	1–4	
Judge 3—7–8	4–6	2–5	
Judge 4—8–1	5–7	3–6	

Finally, someone who has not previously worked on the schedule should be assigned to check the following points on the postings and the checking chart.

1. Every team is listed.
2. No team debates its own school.
3. No team meets the same team twice.
4. No critic judges his own team.
5. No critic judges the same team twice.
6. No critic judges an affirmative team that his team later meets.

Other things also should be kept in mind in scheduling debate.

1. If entries are numerous, teams can be spaced so that no school meets the same school twice.
2. In a regional or national tournament, teams from the same area or part of the country can be put on the same side of the question so that they will meet opponents they do not ordinarily encounter.
3. If more than one division is scheduled, judges can be alternated from one division to another, so that the judging problem is simplified.
4. Standby judges can be listed on the schedule, if only to make the point that standing by is not the same as having a round off.
5. Judges from participating schools need not be used every round. They will usually leave with pleasant memories of the tournament if hired judges were used to give them some free time.
6. Timekeepers need not be listed on the postings. It often is easier to assign them to rooms just before the rounds, keeping track of the rooms they are in.
7. All changes in postings should be recorded on a copy of the postings that is kept in the master notebook. Frequently, judging changes have to be made, and it may later be necessary to have a record of the teams the changes involved.

INDIVIDUAL EVENTS. As in debate, the first step in scheduling individual events is to assign each participant a code designation. The same school codes are used for each event, but the contestants' numbers should differentiate between events, for example, in extemporaneous speaking, individual numbers might be 1, 2, 3; in oratory, 4, 5, 6; and in oral interpretation, 7, 8, 9.

After the codes have been assigned, a list of all contestants, by code, should be drawn up. To find out how many sections will be necessary for an event, the scheduling chairman simply divides the total number of contestants by the number he would like to have in each section. Six persons per section is generally considered the maximum, although room shortages may push it as high as seven or eight. It is often wise to schedule seven or eight in a section to cope with students dropped from the event at registration.

The scheduling process begins by assigning code numbers to sections for the first round. It is easy to guarantee that persons from the same school will not meet during the first round simply by putting them in different sections but in corresponding speaker positions.

The following, simplified example is based on three rounds of oratory. There are eight schools, and four contestants in a section, and four contestants from each school. Again, the example can be extended for any number of contestants and sections. This system is impractical, however, for a small number of contestants because they would have to meet each other twice or compete against students from their own school.

An increasing number of tournaments are moving towards double entry. That is allowing a student to compete in two events. Two methods are possible for dealing with the scheduling problems that will arise from such a tournament. First, the student must be rotated in such a way that his speaking positions are at least three apart in the two events.

ILLUSTRATION

Round I Oratory	Round I Dramatic
Double Entry A_1	J_1
B_1	K_2
C_2	L_4
D_3	T_1
H_2	Double Entry A_1
V_1	P_1

The second way is more effective if the double entry includes extemp and the problems of extemp drawing. This method is the staggered time schedule.

8:30 a.m. Round I Oratory—Debate—Dramatic—Humorous
8:45 a.m. Draw—Extemp and Impromptu—Round I
9:00 a.m. Round I Impromptu
9:15 a.m. Round I Extemp
9:45 a.m. Round II Oratory—Debate—Dramatic—Humorous
10:15 a.m. Extemp and Impromptu Round II Draw
10:30 a.m. Round II Impromptu
10:45 a.m. Round II Extemp

This procedure would continue for rounds three and four. For the last round of the tournament, one alternative is used in a number of states and that is allowing the extemp speaker to use one of his first three topics for round four. This will bring the total schedule to a conclusion about the same time. The advantage of the latter is that all conclude at about the same hour. The former has the significant advantage of results coming to the tabulations room in a less hectic final rush.

Viewing other routine scheduling situations, the following are examples for oratory.

ROUND I

Section	1	2	3	4	5
	A_1	A_2	H_1	H_2	R_2
	B_2	B_1	J_1	R_1	W_1
	C_1	C_2	K_1	M_1	Y_1
	D_2	D_1	L_1	P_1	D_2
	E_1	E_2	M_2	S_1	Z_1
	F_1	F_2	O_1	T_1	S_2
	G_1	G_2	P_2	V_1	T_2

ROUND II

Section	1	2	3	4	5
	G_1	G_2	P_2	V_1	T_2
	O_1	M_2	T_1	S_2	F_1
	S_1	P_1	Y_1	E_1	E_2
	Z_1	O_2	A_1	D_1	L_1
	A_2	B_2	B_1	K_1	M_1
	C_2	D_2	J_1	R_1	R_2
	F_2	H_1	H_2	W_1	C_1

ROUND III

Section	1	2	3	4	5
	S_1	E_2	P_1	Y_1	F_2
	D_1	Z_1	O_2	A_1	L_1
	C_1	W_1	H_2	H_1	C_2
	G_1	G_2	P_2	V_1	T_2
	B_1	A_2	B_2	M_1	K_1
	R_2	E_1	R_1	J_1	D_2
	T_1	S_2	O_1	F_1	M_2

Notice the change in speaking positions. Also as much as possible with the number of entries, speakers are placed against a wide variety of individual and school competition.

67

Oratory Round III

Section	1	2	3	4	5	6	7	8
	A_1	A_2	A_3	A_4	B_1	B_2	B_3	B_4
	C_3	C_4	D_1	D_2	D_3	D_4	C_1	C_2
	G_1	G_2	G_3	G_4	E_1	E_2	E_3	E_4
	J_3	J_4	H_1	H_2	H_3	H_4	J_1	J_2

The final step in scheduling individual events is to arrange the sections so that the speakers do not appear in the same speaking order each time.

Oratory Round III

Section I	Section II	Section III
H_4	C_3	G_1
E_3	E_4	J_2
C_2	J_1	A_3
A_1	A_2	C_4

Continue the same process for all rounds so that each speaker will speak in three different positions such as first, third, and last.

It is easy to arrange for contestants to speak at the beginning, middle, and end of the section during their three rounds of competition. Also, in extemporaneous speaking it is best to arrange the schedule so that two speakers from the same school are never in the same speaking position. The scheduling chairman thereby avoids the possibility that two members of the same school will draw the same set of topics for their extemporaneous speeches.

The assignment of judges for individual events is a relatively easy task if the tournament offers several events. If three types of events are offered, judges should be assigned to a different event each round, judging sections that have no contestants from their own schools. If fewer events are offered than there are rounds, the scheduling chairman will have to make certain that a judge does not hear his own students and does not judge a contestant more than once.

The schedules for the individual events can be checked by following the same system that was utilized for the debates. Contestants should be listed and checked to make sure that persons do not compete against each other twice and that no one faces someone from his own school. The same criteria should be applied when judging assignments are checked.

Some directors feel it is better simply to post schedules on bulletin boards around the tournament headquarters, so that last-minute changes can be handled easily.

At the completion of the scheduling procedure the scheduling chairman will have, in addition to the postings, a complete list of the competition and judging assignments. The judges can then be told the times at which they will be expected to judge. The judging list should be kept in the master notebook and should be kept up to date throughout the contest.

POWER-MATCHING. In such tournaments as the best-record contest, the winners are the teams or individual contestants that have the best records at the end of the competition; however, because ties often occur in such situations, many tournament directors turn to power-matching. In power-matching the best contestants are matched against each other in the later rounds. This ensures that ties will not result and it also provides a better balance of competition throughout the schedule.

To power-match debate, the scheduling chairman sets up, say, the first four rounds in the normal way; then, after the results of the four rounds, are in he can then set up the fifth round. Undefeated teams meet undefeated teams, teams with one loss meet each other, and so on, through the schedule. The sixth round can then be set up on the basis of the fifth round. A clear-cut winner often emerges, as the only undefeated team.

However, this is not always true. To be more sure of a clear-cut winner one needs to power-match after each two rounds. Depending on the size of the tournament and the size of the scheduling crew, the time allocated should be from forty-five minutes to slightly over one hour. Inexperienced directors would be well-advised to avoid this added scheduling "headache" until they have several tournaments "under their belt."

Individual events usually are power-matched only in the last round. The scheduling chairman selects the six or seven persons who have the best rankings and puts them in the same section for the last round. The winner in this section is the winner of the contest. However, because power-matching in individual events amounts to establishing a "hidden final round," many experienced tournament managers prefer to offer a regular final round after the normal competition has been completed. In this way he can be sure that the contestants are at their best, and he can use at least three of his best critics to help decide the winner.

DIRECTING THE COMPETITION

Many operations must be completed between the time events are scheduled and contestants registered and the time that the results are tabulated. This section discusses some of the techniques that have been used to complete these operations.

GENERAL MEETING. Most tournament directors schedule a general meeting before the actual competition begins. At this meeting—one of the few opportunities the contest manager will have to talk to all of the coaches and contestants at once—the guests can be welcomed to the contest by the appropriate school official and by the director of the tournament. Then they can be told the rules, regulations, procedures, and all other data that apply to the contest. The general meeting also is a good time to answer both unexpected and anticipated questions. The contestants can be told where the postings will be placed, where the rooms are, and the rules for the use of the rooms. Finally, they can be informed of any changes that have been made in the tournament at the last minute.

POSTING THE SCHEDULES OF COMPETITION. Although some tournament managers duplicate the postings for the events and put them in the packets that are given out at registration, other directors feel it is better simply to post the schedules on bulletin boards around the tournament's headquarters. Posting only in a central place has advantages. If last-minute changes are necessary, they can easily be made on the three or four copies that have been posted.

The problem with such posting is the congested pushing mass of humanity that surges toward such posting each round. Schedules may well be duplicated for one day at a time and passed out at the commencement of the day. The general attitude of many debaters is the ease of moving and the time and effort expended returning for posting is well worth the chance of someone thinking about who they debate in a later round.

If the tournament is power-matched, either by human or computer means, schedules can either be photo-copied and handed out or posted in pre-determined locations.

In some situations, of course, it is not practical to post round by round in a central place. If a contest is extremely large and the rooms are scattered about the campus, it is unreasonable to expect contestants to return to headquarters after every round. The authors, however, strongly recommend that an inexperienced tournament manager avoid making duplicate postings—until he has enough experience to know that they contain no mistakes. It is far better to post a few accurate, up-to-date schedules in every building than to have mistakes in duplicated schedules and no way of informing the contestants of inadvertent errors.

After the director has run his tournament several times, he will know if it is better to duplicate his schedules. If his contest is "compact" and easy to handle, perhaps he will be able to distribute a complete packet of materials at the beginning of the tournament.

EXTEMPORANEOUS SPEAKING TOPICS. Although the tournament director should have a committee that will have developed a set of topics for extemporaneous speaking, he should make a last-minute check of the topics before he uses them. Are they timely, and do they meet the requirements set forth in the rules, for the event? Do they clearly define the topic areas for the contestants? Are they too easy, or too difficult? Are they serious enough, warranting the contestants and critics' time in dealing with them? If some topics do not meet these criteria, it is better to eliminate them before they are used. A few bad topics can ruin the reputation of a contest.

Probably the easiest way of handling extemporaneous speaking topics is to duplicate all of the topics for a particular round and distribute the complete set to all of the contestants. Each contestant, then, can find the three topics from which he must choose under the number of his speaking position. A list of topics should include at least ten more topics than students will draw (i.e. if thirty students are listed for drawing forty topics should be available).

Many tournament managers, however, prefer and employ a more difficult method. They stagger the drawing times so that all contestants have an equal amount of time in which to prepare for their events. Someone simply calls out the speaker-position numbers at seven- or eight-minute intervals and the contestants come forward to get their topics.

One of the best ways to get good representative topics is to require each school to submit ten or fifteen with their entry. From this list, the host school can add or subtract until a good master list is compiled.

HANDLING THE BALLOTS. The way the ballots for the individual events and debate are handled can have a great influence on the tournament as a whole, and particularly on the tabulations. Steps can be taken that minimize the number of errors that appear in the completed ballots, and the ballots themselves can be used to keep track of the progress of the tournament.

Tournament managers can avoid many problems by seeing that the ballots are carefully prepared. The ballots should be filled in with the names of the judges, the room numbers, the time of each event, and the round number; then envelopes should be made up that have this information on their fronts. If this is done before the ballots are distributed, the tournament director can then be sure that the tabulations chairman will know where every completed ballot has come from. Many inexperienced contest directors have wasted valuable time trying to determine the proper event or debate for an unidentified ballot. Critics cannot always be counted on to fill out their ballots completely. If staffing is adequate, team numbers and sides should be on the debate ballots.

The next step in handling the ballots is distributing them to the judges. An official should sit at the judges' table, with the stack of ballots (in their envelopes) and a copy of the postings. As the ballots are distributed, they should be checked off against the postings. This provides a double check, on judges who have appeared for their assignments and on assignments that have not yet been taken care of. If timekeepers are used to deliver the ballots for each round, they should be instructed to return to tournament headquarters if a judge does not appear after ten minutes. A standby judge can then be sent to fill in for the missing judge.

At the completion of a round, the incoming ballots should again be checked off on a copy of the postings, and missing ballots can then be traced to the corresponding judges. It also is helpful to open each ballot as it comes in to make sure that the critic filled it out completely. It is not unusual that even an experienced judge forgets to include speaker points, or even the winner of the debate. If the ballots are checked immediately, problems can be corrected while the critics are still at the judges' tables or before the tournament draws close to conclusion.

After all of the ballots are checked in, they should be taken to the tabulations room for recording. If the judges' table crew has done its job properly, the persons working in the tabulations room should be able to tabulate the results without worrying about lost or incomplete ballots.

TABULATING TOURNAMENT RESULTS

After all of the ballots have been turned in and checked to see if the information requested on the ballot is properly filled out, they are ready to go to the tabulations room so that the results can be recorded. The six steps in the tabulations process are (1) recording the results, (2) checking for accuracy, (3) distributing the ballots to school results envelopes, (4) recording the results on the summary stencil, (5) rechecking the recording process for accuracy, and (6) determining the winners.

Most tabulation staffs use larger poster boards, divided into several columns, for the initial recording of results. The first column contains the code number of the speaker or team; the other columns represent each round of competition, and allow space for the necessary information that must be transferred from the ballots to the board. A debate tabulations poster contains the following information. The tabulation sheet must contain the division such as A–B or championship–novice, etc.

DEBATE RESULTS DIVISION

Team	Round I	Round II	Round III	Round IV	Total
Code	Win/loss	Win/loss	Win/loss	Win/loss	
No.	Rating	Rating	Rating	Rating	
Code	Win/loss	Win/loss	Win/loss	Win/loss	
No.	Rating	Rating	Rating	Rating	

Most tabulators have found that the win/loss record and rating is sufficient for announcing the winner of an event. Some officials, however, prefer to expand the chart and include the names of the teams, the judges, and individual speaker points. It is good in non-elimination tournaments to provide the codes of schools debated for use in breaking ties.

Individual events results can be tabulated on much the same kind of board or chart.

INDIVIDUAL EVENTS RESULTS

Entrant	Round I		Round II		Round III		Total
Code	Ranking/	over	Ranking/	over	Ranking/	over	
No.	rating	number of	rating	number of	rating	number of	
		contestants		contestants		contestants	

The pertinent information from the ballots usually is recorded on the tabulations charts by teams of two persons. One can call off the information while the other puts the data on the chart. An efficient method for double checking the results uses a clear, plastic chart that duplicates the categories. Another team of tabulators can record the information from the ballots on the plastic sheet, which is placed on top of the original charts so that discrepancies immediately become obvious. No matter how it is done, good tabulation depends upon checking and double checking at all points of the process.

After the tabulations team abstracts the ballots from a particular round, it puts them in separate envelopes for each school. It is strongly recommended that these envelopes be made up ahead of time—so that the copy of the ballot that goes to each school can be placed in the school's envelope as soon as the information has been recorded. The results at many tournaments have been late for the final assembly simply because the tabulations team neglected to

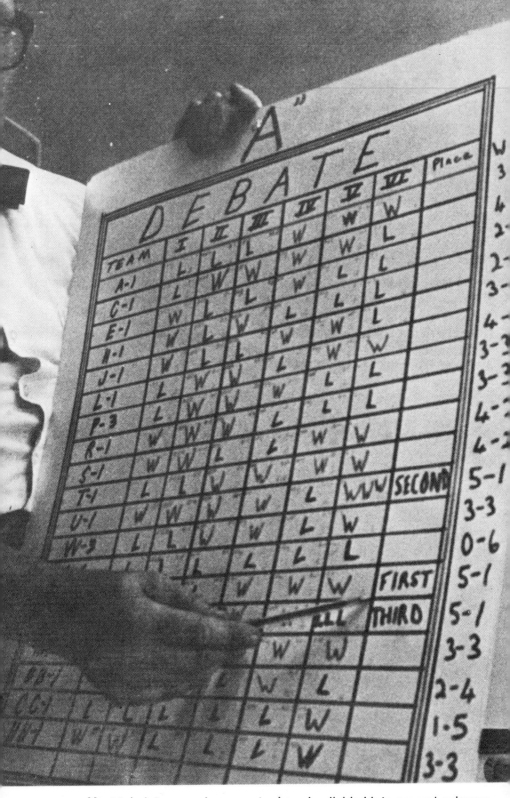

Most tabulators use large poster boards, divided into several columns,
for the initial recording of results.

keep the school envelopes up to date.

Because most tournament directors like to insert a "dittoed" summary of results in the school envelopes, the tabulations crew usually is responsible for keeping a master record of the results. Most tabulators simply abstract the large charts in a duplicating stencil. This, too, is a task that must be kept up to the minute. Generally, the large chart can be given to a typist for preparation during the slack period, while the rounds are going on and the tabulators have no ballots to record.

Final checking takes place when the data on the charts are compared with those of the summary-sheet master. All discrepancies must be corrected because the summary sheet is the contestants' gauge for the accuracy of the tabulations.

After the last round of competition and after the last ballots have been recorded, the tabulations staff is ready to announce the winners of each event, which is easily determined from the tabulations' chart. Debate winners are determined first, from the win/loss records. Obviously, the team with the best record is awarded first place, and so on through the number of places for which there are awards.

The same procedure is used for selecting the top eight or sixteen teams for elimination rounds in the championship elimination tournament.

The winners of individual events are those who score the *lowest* total on the rankings; that is, three first-place rankings totals only three points. In case of a tie, the next criterion is the speaker ratings. Some tabulators break further ties on the basis of the quality of the competition, or they may give two awards instead of one.

TIE BREAKER
DEBATE

	Round I	Round II	Round III	Round IV
TEAM A	W/7/22 E	W/8/20 S	W/9/18 G	W/10/20 E
	24	26	17	20
TEAM B	W/1/26 E	W/2/21 S	W/3/20 G	W/4/15 G
	20	27	15	15

By opponent's strength one would check each opponent's record, i.e. 7-8-9-10 and 1-2-3-4 only for the team debated from that school. If seven won three, eight won two, nine won two, and ten won three, the opponent's strength would be ten. If one won one, two won three; three won two; and four won three, opponents strength would be nine. In this case, Team A would win. If the strength was tied, the next method could be either team rating (column four) or speaker points (column three). In the former case, giving a four for superior,

An efficient tool for double checking results is a plastic chart that duplicates categories.

Envelopes should be made up ahead of time, so that a copy of the ballot can be deposited as soon as it is recorded.

three for excellent, two for good, and one for fair, Team A would have twelve and Team B eleven. In speaker points Team A would have 177 and Team B 158. So in all three methods Team A would be declared the winner. A final method would be if the teams have met, the winner of that match should be the tournament winner.

Although this phase of the tabulations should be checked several times by several persons, the final check should be made by the tournament director. He is ultimately responsible for all mistakes. Therefore, he will want to make sure that none was made.

Determining the results in festivals is somewhat different and easier. The festival director need only select levels that entrants must attain in order to receive certificates of superior and excellent performance. The levels, moreover, tend to be broad and loosely defined, so that many students receive a certificate at the end of the festival.

In the individual events tournament, ties may be broken in either of the two ways illustrated here.

TIE BREAKER

INDIVIDUAL EVENTS

The quickest and simplest method of tie-breaking in individual events is on the basis of the number of contestants spoken against.

Speaker A	1/7	2/8	1/5	1/5	5/25
Speaker B	1/8	2/8	1/6	1/5	5/27

Speaker B is the winner.

The second way is by ratings. This has the advantage of being more accurate in selecting winners.

Speaker A	1/7 90	2/8 92	1/6 90	1/5 89	361
Speaker B	1/7 88	2/8 90	1/6 91	1/5 89	358

Speaker A is the winner.

Here again educational and motivational values are placed much higher in priority than the value of "winning." The giving of many certificates, within the framework we previously illustrated, provides a degree of competitiveness, but serves to highly motivate and educate more students in terms of positive reinforcement.

Many tournaments feature a sweepstakes award that is presented to the school with the best overall record, but several questions must be answered in determining how points should be weighted and awarded. If the emphasis is on debate, more points should be awarded for winning this event than for winning others. If the emphasis is on total participation, in all events, there should be fairly equal assignment of points for the various events. Most contest directors agree that sweepstakes points should not be awarded for anyone who finishes lower than third place; otherwise, the tendency might be to reward quantity participation rather than quality of performance.

However, there are schools, states, and regions who wish to recognize the quantity of good competition and award points in a manner to achieve this end. It is in essence a hybrid of good qualitative performance and quantitative within the limits of the total number of contestants permitted per school.

This type of method is usually followed in that latter format:

Debate win ... ... 8 points
Debate loss ... ... 2 points
First in an individual event round ... ... 4 points
Second in an individual event round ... 3 points
Third in an individual event round... ... 2 points
Fourth or lower in an individual events
round ... ... 1 point

Variations of the points, of course, occur based on what events are stressed in the particular tournament.

The sweepstakes award, of course, is presented to the school with the highest total of points.

THE FINAL ASSEMBLY. The final assembly should be as short and topical as possible. Even the least competitive contestants are interested primarily in the tournament's results, and guests are in no mood to hear lengthy speeches or long discussions of how much work the tournament was and how much credit everyone deserves. Too many contest managers sound like Oscar winners as they spiel off the list of those to whom they are indebted for the success of the contest.

The best procedure is simply to read the names of the award winners, beginning—for dramatic purposes—with the lowest awards and working toward the first place in each event. The sweepstakes award usually is given last, to the coach, student president, or designated student leader of the contestants.

After the awards have been given, the school envelopes should be distributed. When the contestants examine the ballots and summary sheets, the work of the tournament director is almost finished.

MISCELLANEOUS REMARKS. Almost as soon as the tournament is over, the contest manager should inspect his master notebook and make sure that it contains all of the important material that was used in the contest. He should note all experiences, observations, and suggestions that might be helpful in later tournaments. This is a big step toward planning next year's contest.

Immediately after the tournament, the manager should call the newsroom of the local newspaper, which probably will want to publish the tournament's results, and the local wire service office—so that the hometown newspapers of the winners can get the results for their next editions. Most guests are gratified by having attended a tournament important enough to have been reported at home.

Finally, the tournament manager should call a meeting of his entire staff to hear their suggestions for future contests and to thank them for their work on the contest just finished. Such courtesies are not only proper, they are nice ways of ensuring good relationships for future tournaments.

CONCLUDING REMARKS

Good contest managers and good contests have many points in common, which can be summed up in the following advice.

1. *Keep calm.* Control, or at least the appearance of control, should be maintained at all times.
2. *Keep on schedule.* Every effort should be made to start each event on time. "Catch up" times should be scheduled, however, so that there will be time to get back on schedule if contestants or judges are late.
3. *Offer good, well-matched competition.* Schools of relatively equal caliber should be invited. Experienced contestants are discouraged by weak competition and beginners are frightened if they are pitted against those who obviously are veterans.
4. *Give coaches free periods if they are used as judges.* This is an excellent way to win friends for the tournament. An attractive lounge and free refreshments should be offered so that standby judges will be easy to find.
5. *Announce results on time.* People don't mind waiting until 6.00 p.m. if the results were scheduled for announcement at 6.00 p.m. However, ample time should be provided between the last round and the final assembly.
6. *Be accurate.* All tabulations should be checked and double checked.
7. *Be complete.* A complete summary of results should be provided and no information about tabulations, nor any other part of the tournament, should be withheld at the end of the contest. Prior to that time, however, no information should be released from the tabulation room.

CHAPTER V

Ethical Problems in Forensics

Ethical problems, too, confront the tournament director and his choice of the type of format to use may be part of the problem or its cause.

An illustration of a valuable educational experience is the non-trophy tournament. There is some reason to argue that too much emphasis on winning has led to excesses.

"The medium is the message," Marshall McLuhan contends, while many profess to believe that rioters, criminals, and non-conformists in our Society are endeavoring to tell us something through their chosen media. Debaters, too, have their media and it appears that they also are trying to tell us something. Discovering and interpreting this message is one of the most vital tasks confronting the speech profession at this moment.

After years of professional upgrading, better coaching, more time for forensics, higher standards academically, and continued emphasis on high ethical standards, the ethical problem appears to be more intractable than ever. It is past time that we act upon the message we are receiving from debaters in terms of the continued violations of accepted ethical standards. As a part of this action, we must evaluate the meaning of this communication in terms of our teaching and coaching.

Prompted by these urgent considerations and a desire to explore the degree of frequency and significance of the problem, this investigator carried out a study of debaters' practices and their revealed cognitive processes relating to these activities. Data revealed the extent to which debaters, themselves, admitted fabricating evidence or sources and the frequency with which they knowingly used quotations out of their intended contextual meaning. The date also revealed the degree of personal acceptance of these unethical techniques as measured by scales ranging from completely ethical to completely unethical concerning each matter. The procedure of the study was to administer a questionnaire to college debaters at the Heart of America Tournament, held at the University of Kansas, and the invitational tournament held at the United States Naval

Academy. A pre-test was administered before the competition began, and a post-test was given at the conclusion of the elimination rounds to determine whether a significant difference in reporting would occur after intense competition. The debaters were asked to mark a continuum on a one-to-five scale representing the degree to which they practiced such tactics and the degree to which they considered such activities to be ethical. The five point scales ranged from "never done" to "always done" and from "completely ethical" to "completely unethical."

The first finding of the experiment was the result that no significant difference occurred in the responses before and after tournament debates. Based on this data, it is logical to conclude that the message which debaters are attempting to convey to us is the same before, during, and after competition. We would have to conclude that it is not a phenomenon brought on by the heat of conflict or a spur of the moment stimulus.

Eighty-one percent of the respondents indicated that to varying degrees they used material and quotations out of rightful context. In an effort to determine how frequently they followed this procedure, a mean was computed. For all subjects, including the nineteen percent who marked never, the mean score was found to be 2.28. The range was from 1.00 for never to 5.00 for always. Fifty-two per cent of the students responded that they used fabricated evidence or sources. Again the degree varied from 1.25 to 5.00 on the above-mentioned scale. The mean score of the subjects reporting personally fabricating material was 2.34.

On the issue of the ethics concerned, seventy per cent of the debaters surveyed concluded that the practice of taking quotations out of their intended context was somewhere between completely ethical and somewhat ethical. Less than one third (30%) felt that such a practice was totally unethical. The mean score of all s' disclosed a 2.23 score on the ethical-unethical scale. Even more difficult to comprehend was the date revealing that in the opinion of forty-nine per cent of the subjects participating in this study it was to some degree ethical to fabricate material and/or sources.

The major question that we must confront squarely is what is the implication of these findings for our profession. What is the message that these highly intelligent your people are trying to convey to us?

It would be comforting to conclude that this issue simply is a manifestation of a modern phenomena springing from causes entirely unrelated to the forensics' program or the field of speech.

We could argue that cheating incidents have caused major academic scandals at many institutions, that athletic recruiting has led to shady financial practices in our colleges, or that our entire country is covered with the disease of dishonest practices from the high levels of government to the lowest dregs of society. All of these statements would ring with a certain degree of truth, but if we stop at this point we are shirking our responsibility as educators to analyze what our programs can do to prevent such self-destructive behavior.

There can be no secret that a great emphasis on winning trophies, certificates, books, honors, and berths in future desirable tournaments tows in its wake the seeds of dishonesty.

It is not difficult for us to follow the reasoning that the luster of national ratings, bowl bids, conference championships, and post season playoffs has increased the recruiting pressure that has led to the ethical headaches for our colleagues in the athletic department. Why, then, can we not follow good Aristotelean logic to the same conclusion about our own problems? As we continue to pile high-sounding titles on a multiplicity of tournaments, add to the size and number of awards offered, and emphasize, by word and deed, that the ultimate end is in attaining these tangible goals, how can we deny our role in the web of circumstances that has led students to use unethical means to reach the prize set before them?

Never having been in the ranks of the detractors of the award system in the past, it was a difficult step for this writer to conclude that a new look at our tournament structure must be taken—*now*. Athletic associations and conferences have tried sanctions, penalties, and even suspension; but their standards continue to be violated. As long as the reward is worth risking getting caught, human nature seems to be willing to sell out for the mess of pottage. To totally eradicate the incentive seems to be the only effective alternative. We must go the one stop beyond penalties and revise our basic tournament structure and forensic philosophy. Debate must become what we have always felt it was: a teaching and learning device unrivaled in preparing young people for logical thinking and capable speaking.

Development of a tournament structure to fit such a purpose will not be difficult from the mechanical standpoint. However, it must be uniformly adopted; or the urge will still drive many to the win-oriented meet. The problem in establishing such a program will be the emotional response of those of us who have become ingrained with the present policies. It will be easy to attempt to rationalize away the incongruity that the data of this experimental study will create in our minds. Festinger's cognitive dissonance theory gives us a basis for understanding the process that such information evokes. As Festinger has concluded, however, the dissonance can best be removed by accepting the new reality that in this case we have before us in a quantified state and then moving to meet the challenge that this new conception poses for us.

The solutions that seem most logical in terms of maintaining the values of tournament competition are relatively simple. They are equally easy to administer. The ranking approach could be used where each team is evaluated as poor, fair, good, or superior. This system could be based either on an absolute scale or a comparative scale based on a given round. Another alternative would be to retain the won-loss decision, but compile no standings nor give any awards: This methodology might help offset any possible loss of incentive to do the best possible debating. To the old argument that this type of approach will destroy the student's interest, I would respond that our product can and should stand on its academic merits based on its benefits offered to the student.

The results of this study may be gainsaid, but it is time we moved to solve the problem that we knew intuitively we faced; a problem which is now confirmed by this data. If we do not at least proceed with further investigation and action, it is likely another Plato will rightfully rise up to attack the "false rhetoric."

Another ethical problem that may arise during the tournament is the question of "scouting." The tournament director may be confronted with the allegation that someone is using a spare person to go listen to future opponents and copy down their case. Here again the emphasis on winning needs to be examined. However, it is general practice in much of the country to prohibit such scouting.

In individual events, an ethical question that has arisen lies in the area of changing the meaning or the intent of an author in an interpretation. One state speech league has just passed a specific rule that any such practice is banned. The tournament director may be faced with this type of ethical question as well.

A third area that may plague the tournament director is that of judge protests. A coach may, for whatever reason, decide to protest a particular individual assigned to judge his team. The director then might have to decide how any and all of these protests shall be decided.

Some areas of the country have official N.F.L. or state speech league district committees that will assist or adjudicate such disputes at regular season tournaments. A second alternative practice is to have a tournament committee whose job it is to decide such protests and ethical questions. Both of these alternatives make the best of a bad situation. However, the worst alternative is for the director and/or his staff to make the decision. It is much better to have someone else calmly and judiciously determine the matter.

The final ethical point would be the bringing of unethical conduct charges, during a round, against an individual or team. Here again, the above discussed committees and possibly changed formats may aid in alleviating the hostility involved.

Another problem that a tournament director may face is the case of error when awards are announced. The best of a bad alternative, again, is simply the giving of alternative awards.

An incorrect decision by a judge on a ballot can most generally be corrected the same way or by catching the judge before the final round and then he may correct the error himself.

All of these protests and problems arise from the aforementioned emphasis on winning and trophies. Not only have we suggested practical expedients for immediate solutions, but we believe a long range possibility is suggested. Thus, the tournament director must provide a machinery for dealing with protests and unethical conduct.

APPENDIX

SECTION I

Tournament Director's Master Notebook

The master notebook is a collection of all the material that is relevant to a particular tournament or festival. The contest director should file the materials, as he gets them, in clearly marked sections of the notebook. If he organizes his master notebook well and keeps it up to date, he will find that this method is almost indispensable for preparing and managing a successful contest.

We believe the organization suggested on these pages is the most practical, but the important thing is that the tournament director develop a notebook system that fits his needs. Regardless of the organizational system he uses, various materials undoubtedly will appear in all master notebooks. The material that follows, in four sections, is a collection of references and sample materials that the authors have found very useful in directing tournaments.

SECTION I: PREPARATIONS FOR THE TOURNAMENTS
Sample Preliminary Announcement
Verification of Registration Form
Fee Schedule and Registration Card
Sample Final Announcement
Sample Extemporaneous Speaking Topics

SECTION II: SCHEDULING AND POSTING
Time Chart for the Tournament
Master List of Available Rooms
Master Chart for Events
Encoder
Scratch Sheet
Sample Postings for Debate
Sample Postings for an Individual Event

SECTION III: TABULATION OF RESULTS
Sample Oratory Chart
Sample Debate Chart
Sample Summary of Results

SECTION IV: JUDGES AND TIMEKEEPING
Debate Judging Instructions
Oratory Judging Instructions
Extemporaneous Speaking Judging Instructions
Oral Interpretation Judging Instructions
Instructions for Timekeepers and Chairmen
Master List of Qualified Judges and Their Assignments
Payment Sheet for Judges
Master List of Timekeepers

CHECKLIST FOR TOURNAMENTS
Tournament Staff

Assistant Tournament Manager

Name:................................   Phone:.................................

Registration and Hosting Chairman

Name:................................   Phone:.................................

Rooms and Facilities Chairman

Name:................................   Phone:.................................

Judges Chairman

Name:................................   Phone:.................................

Tabulations Chairman

Name:................................   Phone:.................................

Events Scheduling Chairman

Name:................................   Phone:.................................

Timekeeper's Chairman

Name:................................   Phone:.................................

Tournament Announcement

Number sent:................   Date mailed:................   Deadline:................

Confirmation of Entry Letters Sent (Optional)

School:................................   Date:................................

Materials and Equipment List:

Item ordered:................   Cost:................   Delivery date................

Preparations for the Tournament

SAMPLE PRELIMINARY ANNOUNCEMENT

This form announces the contest, provides information about the events and their rules, stipulates the fee schedule, and informs the prospective participants about the time schedule. It should be mailed well in advance of the tournament.

THIRTY-SEVENTH ANNUAL
ROCKY MOUNTAIN SPEECH CONFERENCE TOURNAMENT

High School Division

Department of Speech, University of Denver
February 10 and 11, 1968

Dear Director of Forensics:

We extend a cordial invitation to you and your squad to participate in the Thirty-Seventh Annual Rocky Mountain Speech Conference Tournament.

You will notice that this year's tournament will use a "championship" format with elimination finals in all events. There will be five preliminary rounds of debate plus semi-finals and finals. There will be two preliminary rounds and a final round in all individual events.

The R.M.S.C. is again being held in downtown Denver, utilizing the facilities of the University of Denver Business Administration Campus.

Please return your entry form by *January 31, 1968*. We are anticipating a large entry and will not be able to guarantee participation of all schools. We are able to confirm only the *first* 60 teams reserving places; so get your entry in early and you will receive confirmation of your entries soon after the January 31 deadline.

Cordially,

Roy V. Wood, Ph.D.
Director of Forensics

Steven Hunt and John Walker
Tournament Directors

A SAMPLE LIST OF RULES

1. Each school may send up to 12 entries.
2. This may include no more than three debate teams.
3. Students may double enter.
4. No more than six in individual events.
5. Sweepstakes shall be computed based on the school's entry finishing HIGHEST in each event eliminating the LOWEST event.
6. One judge shall be required for each five entries or fraction thereof. Schools traveling over 300 miles, one way, may reduce this by one judge. Each judge shall judge at least three rounds each day.
7. Six preliminary debate rounds in each division—eliminations start with octafinals. Three preliminary rounds in Extemp, Original Oratory, and Dramatic. Eliminations start with quarter finals.
8. Debate will be cross-examination, two-man, switch-sides.
9. Teams that are 15 minutes late for a round may forfeit that round. Judges 15 minutes late may cause a forfeit against their team that round.

The Advisory Committee Room will be in 301, Libbey Hall.

VERIFICATION OF REGISTRATION FORM

This form should be mailed to all whose entries have been accepted, just after the deadline for entering the contest and one or two weeks prior to the contest date. It reminds the entrants of the number of entries, the fees, and any last-minute information.

School ....

Coach ....

No. of Debate teams..

No. of entrants in extemporaneous speaking...

No. of entrants in oratory..

No. of entrants in interpretation..

Fees due..

Welcome to the tournament! We hope to make this the best conference ever. This cannot be done if too many last-minute changes are made. If you have unavoidable changes, *please* wire or telephone us at the earliest possible moment.

Office phone — 753–2301 or 753–2385

Home phone — 756–5800

If you plan to arrive by public transportation, let us know so we can meet you and take you to your hotel.

FEE SCHEDULE AND REGISTRATION CARD

This card should be prepared by the contest manager or by the assistant in charge of fees or scheduling. It serves as the official registration card and as notification of the official fees for each school. If the code numbers for contestants are included, this card becomes a summary of all the pertinent data for the visiting coach.

SCHOOL ....   Fees due $..........................

COACH ....   Paid in full

JUDGE...
....
Tournament Director

DEBATE TEAM No. 1...........................

EXTEMP. (Names of Students)   ....

1. ....

2. ....   DEBATE TEAM No. 2...........................

3. ....

4. ....

ORATORY (Names of Students)   ORAL INTERPRETATION

1. ....   1. ....

2. ....   2. ....

3. ....   3. ....

4. ....   4. ....

A copy of this final registration card can serve as a receipt and list of entries for the visiting coach.

SAMPLE FINAL ANNOUNCEMENT

The information contained in the final announcement should include all that the contestants and coaches will have to know during the tournament. Some information is simply copied from the preliminary announcement; other information is added just for this announcement. This announcement should be included in the packet each visiting school receives during the registration period.

REVISED SCHEDULE

February 9

6.00 p.m. to 9.00 p.m. .... Registration,
Business Adm. Bldg.,
1445 Cleveland Place,
Downtown Denver.

February 10

9.00 a.m. to noon .... Registration (as above)

Noon .... Extemp. Draw

12.30 p.m. .... Extemp. I, Oratory I

1.30 p.m. .... Extemp. Draw

2.00 p.m. .... Interp. I, Extemp. II

3.15 p.m. .... Interp. II, Oratory II

4.30 p.m. .... Debate I

5.45 p.m. .... Debate II

7.00 p.m. .... Extemp. Draw for Finals

7.30 p.m. .... Finals All Individuals

February 11

8.30 a.m. .... Debate III

9.45 a.m. .... Debate IV

11.00 a.m. .... Debate V

1.00 p.m. .... Results and Awards

1.30 p.m. .... Semi-Final Round

2.45 p.m. .... Final Round

SAMPLE EXTEMPORANEOUS SPEAKING TOPICS

The topics should be prepared by a committee assigned this job by the contest manager well before the actual contest date. Extemporaneous speaking topics should be current and of real interest to the students who will be using them. They should be challenging, but not obscure. Only one main idea should be included in each topic. The topic should suggest a frame of reference from which the contestant can construct his speech. These topics can be chosen from an envelope or from a prepared list.

EXTEMPORANEOUS QUESTIONS

1. Why did the Republicans win two more governships?
2. Was Gallup correct in showing Nixon's policy speech approved by 77%?
3. Is inflation on the way out?
4. What is the meaning of Lindsay's victory in New York?
5. Can cities survive?
6. Is the taxpayer's revolt for real?
7. Is Spiro Agnew an asset to the Nixon Administration?
8. What is the real Clement Haynesworth?
9. Foreign Aid—Will it be cut again?
10. Will the war in Vietnam end?
11. How will the war in Vietnam end?
12. Is the new West German government pro-Western?
13. What is the role of dissent in the modern school?
14. Should 19 year olds vote?
15. Is George Wallace still a major threat?
16. Is the New South the new Republican majority?
17. Will Hugh Scott be an effective Republican leader?
18. Should the Kopechne case be aired further?
19. How does the Kopechne case affect Edward Kennedy's political future?
20. Whose side is Hubert Humphrey on?
21. Who really is the leader of the Democrats?
22. Will the draft lottery work?
23. Ahead a volunteer army?
24. How can sky jackings be stopped?
25. What is the effect of the Nixon Latin American policy?
26. What is the future of Laos?
27. Will revenue sharing work?
28. Will the Nixon welfare plan really help?
29. Is the Nixon legislative program likely to succeed?

Scheduling and Posting

TIME CHART FOR THE TOURNAMENT

This chart is a planning device. It can be used by the contest manager to keep track of the time schedule just before the tournament. When will the rounds be scheduled? When will the schedules be posted? At what time should the results have been tabulated?

Time	"Meeting Up Rounds"	Posting	Tabulation Duties

Master List of Available Rooms

This list should be maintained by the room chairman. He can use it to double check the rooms in the building to make sure they are actually available at the times they have been scheduled. A copy of the list should be passed on to the person in charge of scheduling.

Building	Room No.	Hours Available	Special Information

MASTER CHART FOR EVENTS

This list can be used by the scheduling chairman to make certain that events will not conflict unexpectedly. It also can serve as a check against two events being scheduled for the same room.

Time   Event   Room

_____

_____

_____

_____

_____

_____

_____

_____

_____

_____

_____

_____

_____

_____

_____

_____

_____

_____

ENCODER

All schools entered in the contest should be listed on this chart; then code letters can be assigned to them. Naturally, such a list is necessary for the preparation of the materials to be handed out at registration. It also is valuable later, when it can be used as the list of the individual contestants and the teams in each event. It should be prepared by the scheduling chairman prior to the actual scheduling process.

Code	School	Location
A		
B		
C		
D		
E		
H		
K		
L		
M		
N		
P		
R		
S		
T		
U		
W		
X		
Y		
Z		
AA		
BB		

SCRATCH SHEET

This sheet has many uses in the master notebook—a scratch sheet for scheduling, for assigning judges, and for assigning timekeepers. If a school, a team, or an individual contestant has dropped out of the tournament, the complete information should be recorded on a scratch sheet. It is best to use a separate sheet for each event and/or division. Using a heavy rule on each fifth line allows for rapid counting.

1.

2.

3.

4.

5.

6.

7.

8.

9.

10.

11.

12.

13.

14.

15.

16.

17.

18.

19.

20.

SAMPLE POSTING FOR DEBATE

A copy of all the postings should be kept in the contest manager's master notebook. All changes in schedules should be recorded on the master copies.

Aff.	Neg.	Judge	Room
KK_1	GG_1	Prosper (C)	207
C_2	JJ_2	Kwehl (D)	215
R_1	PP_1	Grannell (E)	223
S_1	HH_1	Greenagel (G)	224
T_1	G_2	Holley (H)	231
P_1	JJ_1	Stitzel (J)	239
D_2	NN_1	Clay (N)	242
N_2	XX_1	Blair (M)	247
AA_1	FF_1	Dougherty (P)	258
P_2	BB_1	Parson (R)	263
S_2	FF_2	Isenhour (T)	265
C_1	N_1	McGinnis (V)	271
T_2	GG_2	Petelle (W)	307
W_2	M_1	Silvey (X)	313
X_2	NN_2	Sampson (Z)	314
Z_2	XX_2	Aschenbrenner (AA)	315
B_1	G_1	Reyes (BB)	327
W_1	H_2	Dudley (DD)	330
D_1	DD_1	Feather (FF)	335
KK_2	E_1	Walker (HH)	343
Z_1	EE_2	Johnson (JJ)	351

SAMPLE POSTINGS FOR AN INDIVIDUAL EVENT

Copies of the individual events schedules also are kept in the master notebook. These schedules also are posted for the contestants and given to the chairmen of tabulations, judging, and timekeeping.

Section 1 Room 231 Judge: Prosper (B)	Section 2 Room 239 Judge: Dudley (C)	Section 3 Room 242 Judge: Johnson (D)
A_7	B_8	C_8
G_{11}	H_6	J_{11}
E_9	K_6	M_8
R_{10}	U_4	W_7
AA_4	BB_6	KK_7

Section 4 Room 247 Judge: Stitzel (L)	Section 5 Room 263 Judge: McGinnis (P)	Section 6 Room 265 Judge: Silvey (R)
LL_5	D_7	A_8
G_{14}	J_{12}	H_7
P_6	E_{10}	M_9
R_{10}	X_5	Y_6
AA_5	KK_8	

Section 7
Room 351
Judge: Holley (E)

C_9
J_{13}
M_{10}
R_{12}
KK_9

APPENDIX—SECTION III

Tabulation of Results

SAMPLE ORATORY CHART

This tabulation's chart is used in a variety of ways. As a poster board, it is used as the method for recording results and determining awards. It is then copied onto a ditto mat and distributed to the contestants after the contest. A copy also should be placed in the master note book.

Code	Round I	Round II	Round III	Total	Rank
A_8	2/E	4/E	1/S	E–E–S 2–4–1	
A_9	4/G	1/S	4/E	G–S–E 4–1–4	
A_{10}	4/G	2/E	3/E	G–E–E 4–2–3	
B_8	4/G	2/E	4/F	G–E–F 4–2–4	
B_9	4/S	2/S	4/G	S–S–G 4–2–4	
B_{10}	2/S	4/E	2/E	S–E–E 2–4–2	
C_8	4/G	4/F	4/E	G–F–E 4–4–4	
C_{10}	4/F	4/E	3/G	F–E–G 4–4–3	
D_8	2/S	2/S	1/S	S–S–S 2–2–1	
D_9	1/S	2/S	1/S	S–S–S 1–2–1	2nd
D_{10}	3/F	4/E	4/G	F–E–G 3–4–4	
E_8	3/G	4/E	4/E	G–E–E 3–4–4	
E_9	3/G	4/G	4/E	G–G–E 3–4–4	
E_{10}	4/F	3/S	4/E	F–S–E 4–3–4	
F_8	4/E	2/E	3/E	E–E–E 4–2–3	
F_9	3/S	3/E	4/G	S–E–G 3–3–4	
F_{10}	4/G	2/E	1/S	G–E–S 4–2–1	
G_8	4/F	2/S	4/G	F–S–G 4–2–4	
G_9	ns	ns	ns	ns	
G_{10}	1/G	4/E	4/G	G–E–G 1–4–4	

SAMPLE DEBATE CHART

Code	Round I	Round II	Round III	Round IV	Round V	Round VI	Total	Finals
A_1	L/E	L/A	W/S	W/E	L/S	W/A	3–3	
B_1	L/E	L/A	W/S	L/A	W/A	L/A	2–4	
C_1	W/S	L/E	L/S	L/E	L/E	W/A	3–3	
D_1	L/E	W/A	W/S	L/S	W/S	L/S	3–3	
E_1	W/S	W/S	W/S	W/E	W/E	L/S	5–1	1st
F_1	W/E	W/E	L/S	W/S	W/S	L/A	4–2	
G_1	W/E	W/E	L/E	W/E	L/E	L/E	3–3	
H_1	L/A	L/A	L/A	L/F	L/F	L/F	0–6	
K_1	L/E	W/E	W/S	W/S	W/E	W/S	5–1	3rd
L_1	W/E	L/A	L/A	W/E	L/E	L/A	2–4	
M_1	W/E	L/E	W/E	W/S	W/S	L/A	4–2	
P_1	L/A	W/E	L/A	L/A	L/F	W/E	2–4	
R_1	L/A	L/A	L/E	L/A	W/A	W/A	2–4	
S_1	W/A	W/E	W/E	L/E	L/S	W/E	4–2	
T_1	W/A	L/E	L/E	L/A	L/A	L/A	1–5	
Y_1	W/S	W/S	W/S	W/E	L/E	L/A	4–2	
Z_1	L/E	W/A	W/A	W/E	W/S	W/A	5–1	
AA_1	L/A	L/F	L/A	L/A	L/A	W/E	1–5	
BB_1	W/S	W/E	W/E	W/S	L/E	W/S	5–1	2nd
CC_1	W/E	L/S	W/E	L/E	W/S	L/A	3–3	
DD_1	L/E	L/S	L/S	L/S	W/S	W/E	3–3	
EE_1	L/A	L/A	W/E	W/E	W/E	W/E	4–2	
FF_1	W/A	W/S	L/E	L/A	L/E	W/A	3–3	

As previously discussed, it is often wise to add the opponent each round.

SAMPLE SUMMARY OF RESULTS

The summary of results is prepared by the tabulations' chairman. If possible, it should be passed out after the awards ceremony. However, many contest directors mail the summary material after the contest is over.

ORAL INTERPRETATION

1st: North High School	Christine Prokop	1 1 2 2
2nd: Mullen High School	Tom McNally	1 1 2 2
3rd: George Washington	Kay Hunsinger	1 2 2 2

ORATORY

1st: Mt. Carmel	Rosa Soy	1 1 1 2
2nd: Machbeuf	Mary Ann Walsh	1 1 2 2
3rd: Abraham Lincoln	Sharon Stevenson	1 1 2 2

EXTEMPORANEOUS SPEAKING

1st: Boulger High School	Curt Stocker	1 1 1 1
2nd: George Washington	Chris Mills	1 2 1 1
3rd: Cheyenne Central	Peggy Boice	1 2 2 1

DEBATE

1st: Thomas Jefferson 6–0   Joel Friedman–Ron Ellis
2nd: Cathedral High School 5–1 Mike Di Manna–Tom Haney
3rd: Cheyenne Central 4–2   Bobbi Birleffe–Bill Jeffrey

SWEEPSTAKES

1st: Thomas Jefferson 71
2nd: Cheyenne Central 60

Judges and Timekeepers

DEBATE JUDGING INSTRUCTIONS

Prepared well in advance of the tournament, these instructions should be included with the ballots if relatively novice judges are used. Even experienced judges must know the rules that apply to the contests they are judging.

A. Your decision should be based on which team did the better job of debating and not on your personal opinions or convictions. The debaters are debating each other, not the judge. Be objective as you listen to the debate and evaluate the techniques being employed. There is no place in debate judging for subjective evaluation.

B. Try to determine which team establishes the greater probability for their position. The debate should be centered on the significance of the problem based on an analysis of the causes and the desirability and practicality of proposed solutions, as supported by evidence and reasoning.

C. The following outline will help you judge the debate. This is a general prospectus of what should happen:

1. The affirmative will state the proposition and define terms. They will then usually explain the nature of the problem and trace the causes, citing evils in the present situation (the status quo). They will show how their proposed changes will correct the situation and will usually mention certain advantages that will probably come about if their proposal is accepted.

2. The negative will usually defend the status quo and attack the arguments for a change being advanced by the affirmative. They may do this by pointing out that there is no need for a change and that any change would be worse than the present. They may argue that there is no problem or that the problem is presently being solved by changes already in progress.

3. There will usually be several main contentions or major arguments that are of such importance that you can determine who wins the debate by deciding which team won these major arguments.

4. The affirmative may also contend that unique significant comparative advantages over the present system will accrue from their plan. Then they do not have to argue a need or evil.

5. The affirmative may also use a criteria case that any solution must fit and compare how their plan and the status quo do, in fact, meet it.

6. Remember, the affirmative team has the responsibility of establishing the probability that their proposal will correct the evils in the status quo. If they use the comparative advantage approach, they need only show that their plan is comparatively advantageous and does not induce significant new harms. In the criteria case they must show: that the criteria is the best one to judge the situation by and that their plan can more effectively fit it without adding new disadvantages. They will attempt to do this by the quality and quantity of evidence and the soundness of their reasoning as they defend their position.

7. If the negative team uses a counter-plan they must prove that this proposal is based on a legitimate interpretation of the proposition and that it will solve the problem in a better way than the plan advanced by the affirmative.

D. Technical aspects of debate to be considered in judging:

1. There should be agreement on definition of terms as the debate progresses. The affirmative usually defines the terms, but the negative has the right to challenge the definitions, if they feel the affirmative has been unfair in defining terms. Unless the definition of terms is attacked by the negative, the definitions advanced by the affirmative are assumed to be accepted.

2. The construction of the affirmative case should be done early enough in the debate for the negative to attack it. Totally new arguments for or against the proposition should not be introduced so late in the debate (such as in the rebuttal period), that the other team has no chance to deal with the arguments.

3. Arguments must be supported by reasoning and evidence. If arguments are not supported, the opposition should call attention to the fact and insist that the arguments be supported. However, if an argument is advanced and is not dealt with in any way by the opposition, it is presumed to be won by the team advancing the argument.

4. If you as a judge know that evidence is being distorted or that the debaters are being dishonest, you should penalize them

accordingly. You must be very careful in handling this situation and be very sure of your information. (It is better if the opposition can point out misuses of evidence.)

5. Minor infractions of the rules such as going a few seconds overtime, whispering too loudly during the debate, etc., should not unduly influence your decision. In like manner, delivery alone should not determine the winner, since the emphasis should be on the presentation of the arguments. If poor delivery or minor infractions of the rules interfere with the major aspects of the debate, this should be considered in rendering your decision.

6. You should not require either team to meet arguments or issues in your mind that are not advanced successfully by the opposition.

7. A negative team may argue for simple modifications or repairs of the present system.

ORATORY JUDGING INSTRUCTIONS

Like the debate judging instructions, a copy of the instructions for judging individual events should be included with the ballots for those events. A copy of the instructions should be kept in the master notebook for ready reference.

1. Read carefully the criteria listed below, upon which you are to base your decision.

2. After each speaker has finished, offer your critique on one of the sheets provided. Please note the name and school of the speaker so it may be returned to his coach later. *Return this critique sheet to the judges' table.*

3. After the last speaker has finished, keeping the criteria for this event in mind, record your ratings and rankings in the space provided.

4. Double check your decisions to make sure you have recorded exactly what you intended.

5. Return the ballot to the judges' table as soon as possible.

BASES FOR DECISION:

1. Consider the suitability of the subject. Is the subject worthwhile, appropriate, timely?

2. Consider thought content. Is there evidence of critical thinking? Is the approach fresh and challenging?

3. Consider organization. Is the introduction adequate? Are points apparent? Are transitions clear? Is the arrangement effective? Is the conclusion adequate?

4. Consider the development of ideas. Is there an adequate use of repetition, restatement, cumulation, example, illustration and evidence for effective communication?

5. Consider the use of language. Is the wording direct, accurate, vivid, and forceful?

6. Consider voice and diction. Is the voice pleasant and appealing? Is pronunciation acceptable? Is enunciation distinct without being pedantic? Is there enough variety and emphasis?

7. Consider bodily action. Does the speaker have "unobstructive" poise and animation? Is he direct and physically communicative? Does he have distracting habits and mannerisms?

EXTEMPORANEOUS SPEAKING JUDGING INSTRUCTIONS

1. Read carefully the criteria listed below, upon which you are to base your decision.

2. After each speaker has finished, offer your critique on one of the sheets provided. Please note the name and school of the speaker so it may be returned to his coach later. *Return the critique sheets to the judges' table.*

3. After you have written your critique, keeping the criteria for this event in mind, record your rating and rankings in the space provided.

4. Double check your decisions to make sure you have recorded exactly what you intended.

5. *Return the ballot to the judges' table as soon as possible.*

BASES FOR DECISION:

1. Did the speaker demonstrate a knowledge of the topic being considered?

2. Did he select significant ideas and treat them in a meaningful manner?

3. Did he possess the ability to extemporize, to compose his language as he spoke?

4. Was the introduction adequate? Were the main ideas apparent? Were the transitions clear? Was the conclusion adequate?

5. Consider audibility, directness, fluency, poise, and the use of good English.

6. Consider the pertinency, dependability, and sufficiency of the evidence presented.

7. Consider how clearly outlined and easy to follow the speech seemed to be.

ORAL INTERPRETATION JUDGING INSTRUCTIONS

1. Please read carefully the criteria listed below.

2. Write your suggestions and comments for each speaker on the individual critique sheets.

3. After all contestants have spoken, record your rankings and ratings for each contestant on the ballot.

4. Double check your decision to make sure that you have recorded exactly what you intended.

5. Return your ballot to the judges' table as quickly as possible.

CRITERIA

INTRODUCTION
Content: Adequacy of material, style and mood of material in harmony with the selection.
Delivery: Direct, confident, setting the mood.

SELECTION
Content: Appropriate to contestant.
Cutting: Cohesive and consistent with the literary whole from which the cutting was made.
Delivery: Well-prepared, emotionally appropriate, performer well controlled.

VISUAL
Gestures: Movement, facial expression.
Poise: Posture, mannerisms, clothes, confidence, alertness.

AUDIO

Voice and Articulation: Rate, pitch, inflection, force, quality.

Pronunciation: Acceptable syllable stress, acceptable word stress, freedom from substandard pronunciation.

REACTION OF AUDIENCE

Clear imagery: Projection of meaning for understanding, appreciation, and   proper emotional response of audience.

CHARACTERS (For prose and play readings)

Believably created, consistent, interplay among character; characters clearly defined and distinguished. Characters suggested by interpretation rather than by acting.

INSTRUCTIONS FOR TIMEKEEPERS AND CHAIRMEN

These instructions can profitably be included with the sets of time cards that are given the timekeepers before they leave for the debate rounds.

Name   ....

Room ....

1. At the timekeepers' table you will be given a set of time cards that read: 10, 9, 8, 7, 6, 5, 4, 3, 2, 1, $\frac{1}{2}$, STOP. You will also be given your room assignment.

2. Report to the room to which you are assigned at least five minutes before the round is scheduled to begin.

3. How to time events:

  A. Oratory

  (1) Begin with the 10-minute card. After a contestant has spoken for 1 minute, put up the 9-minute card. Continue in this manner until the contestant has 1 minute left to speak. When he has spoken for $\frac{1}{2}$ that time, put up the $\frac{1}{2}$-minute time card. When his time is up, put up the STOP card. Do not stand up. Do not call out "Stop!" Raise your hand when you put this card up. This will serve as a signal to the judge that the contestant's time is up.

  (2) Before the beginning of the round, ask the judge if he would like you to tell him the time each contestant speaks.

(3) We will not supply watches. (Be sure you return the watch if you have to borrow one.)

B. Extemporaneous
(1) Follow the instructions for Oratory *but begin with the seven-minute card.*

C. Oral Interpretation
(1) Follow the instructions for Oratory *but begin with the eight-minute card.*

4. Timing Debate
A. There are eight speeches in debate. The first four speeches are *ten* minutes; the next four are *five* minutes.
B. Follow the instructions for Oratory on the specifics of timing.

5. Be sure to return the time cards to the timekeepers' table.

6. Under NO circumstances are you to reveal to *anyone* any results that you may be aware of. This is imperative for the working of the tournament.

7. We thank you for your cooperation. If you are interested in learning more about the forensics program at the University, please call Professor Terry or Miss Olson at either Ext. 2700 or 2553. You are invited to the next meeting of the debate squad Tuesday in UH 422.

MASTER LIST OF QUALIFIED JUDGES AND THEIR ASSIGNMENTS

This list is used by the chairman in charge of judges. It should be used while the judges are being obtained and as they are assigned to rounds.

Judge	Address and Phone No.	Assignments

PAYMENT SHEET FOR JUDGES

If the judges are being paid, this sheet provides an excellent summary that will help
keep the records straight.

Code No.	Name	Rounds Judged							Amount Due	When paid, verify by signature
		I	II	III	IV	V	VI	Total		

BIBLIOGRAPHY

Baird, A. Craig, *Argumentation, Discussion and Debate*, New York: McGraw-Hill, 1950.

—— *Public Discussion and Debate*, Boston: Ginn and Company, 1939.

Behl, William A., *Discussion and Debate*, New York: Ronald Press, 1953.

Bilsky, Manuel, *Patterns of Argument*, New York: Holt, Rinehart & Winston, 1963.

Braden, Waldo, *Speech, Methods and Resources*, New York: Harper & Row, 1961.

Buys, William, *Speaking by Doing*, Skokie, Ill.: National Textbook Corp., 1967.

Buys, William, Martin, Cobin, Paul Hunsinger, Melvin Miller and Robert Scott, *Contest Speaking Manual*, Skokie, Ill.: National Textbook Co., 1964.

Buys, William, Jack Murphy, and Bruce Kendall, *Discussion and Debate*, Skokie, Ill.: National Textbook Corp., 1966.

Capp, Glenn R., and Thelma Robuck Capp, *Principles of Argumentation and Debate,* Englewood Cliffs, N.J.: Prentice-Hall, 1965.

Chenoweth, Eugene C., *Discussion and Debate,* Dubuque: Wm. C. Brown Publishing Co., 1951.

Courtney, Luther W., Glenn R. Capp, *Practical Debating*, Philadelphia: J. B. Lippincott Co., 1949.

Crocker, Lionel, *Argumentation and Debate*, New York: American Book Co., 1944.

Ehninger, Douglas, and Wayne Brockriede, *Decision by Debate*, New York: Dodd, Mead & Co., 1963.

Ewbank, Henry, and Jeffery Auer, *Discussion and Debate*, New York: Appleton-Century-Crofts, 1946.

Foster, William T., *Argumentation and Debating*, Boston: Houghton Mifflin, 1948.

Freeley, Austin J., *Argumentation and Debate*, Belmont, Calif.: Wadsworth Publishing Co., 1966.

Gulley, Hulbert, *Essentials of Discussion and Debate*, New York: Holt, Rinehart & Winston, 1955.

Hedde, Wilhelmina G., and William N. Brigance, *American Speech*, Philadelphia: J. B. Lippincott Co., 1955.

Hirt, Anne C., *Suggestions for Contest Speaking*, Minneapolis: Northwestern Press, 1954.

Holley, Donald, *Extempore Speaking*, New York: H. W. Wilson Co., 1947.

Holm, J. N., *How to Judge Speech Contests*, Portland, Me.: Platform News Publication Co., 1938.

Huber, Robert B., *Influencing through Argument*, New York: David McKay Co., 1963.

Hunsinger, Paul, *Communicative Interpretation*, Dubuque: Wm. C. Brown Publishing Co., 1967.

Klopf, Donald W., and Carroll P. Lahman, *Coaching and Directing Forensics*, Skokie, Ill.: National Textbook Co., 1967.

McBath, James H., *Argumentation and Debate*, New York: Holt, Rinehart & Winston, 1963.

McBurney, James H., and James M. O'Neill, *Argumentation and Debate*, New York: Macmillan, 1951.

McBurney, James H., and Glen E. Mills, *Argumentation and Debate*, New York: Macmillan, 1964.

Melzer, Arnold, *High School Forensics*, New York: H. W. Wilson Co., 1936.

Mills, Glenn E., *Composing the Speech*, Englewood Cliffs, N.J.: Prentice-Hall, 1952.

Murphy, James J., and Jon M. Ericson, *The Debater's Guide*, Indianapolis: Bobbs-Merrill, 1961.

Musgrave, George McCoy, *Competitive Debate*, New York: H. W. Wilson Co., 1946.

Nichols, Alan, *Discussion and Debate*, New York: Harcourt, Brace & World, 1941.

Nichols, E. R., and J. H. Baccus, *Modern Debating*, New York: Norton, 1936.

Pearson, Paul M., *Extemporaneous Speaking*, New York: Noble & Noble, 1930.

Potter, David (ed.), *Argumentation and Debate*, New York: Dryden Press, 1954.

Shepard, David W., and Paul Cashman, *A Handbook for Beginning Debaters*, Minneapolis: Burgess Publishing Co., 1962.

Rieke, R. D., and D. F. Faules, *Directing Forensics*, Scranton: International Textbook Company, 1968.

Summers, Harrison B., *Contest Debating*, New York: H. W. Wilson Co., 1934.

Summers, Harrison B., and F. L. Wahn, *How to Debate*, New York: H. W. Wilson Co., 1940.

Terry, Donald R., *Modern Debate Case Techniques*, Skokie, Ill.: National Textbook Co., 1970 (available Spring 1970).

Wells, E. W., and P. X. Knoll, *The Extempore Speech*, New York: Ronald Press, 1942.

Wood, Roy V., *Strategic Debate*, Skokie, Ill.: National Textbook Co., 1968.

A Selected List of Books and Materials
For Students and Teachers of Forensics

Klopf, Donald, and Lahman, Carroll P. *Coaching & Directing Forensics*. Skokie, Ill.: National Textbook Corporation, 1967.

Buys, Cobin, Hunsinger, Miller, and Scott. *Contest Speaking Manual*. Skokie, Ill.: National Textbook Corporation, 1964.

Complete Handbook on the National High School Debate Topic. Skokie, Ill.: National Textbook Corporation, published annually.

Buys, William E., Murphy, Jack, and Kendall, Bruce. *Discussion and Debate*. Skokie, Ill.: 1964, with supplement on current national high school debate topic published annually.

Copeland, James M. (ed.). *ISSUES*. Skokie, Ill.: report to advanced debaters published monthly, October through May.

NOTES